COUNTRY TOWN
COLORING BOOK

by TONY CLARK

This Coloring Book Belongs to

____

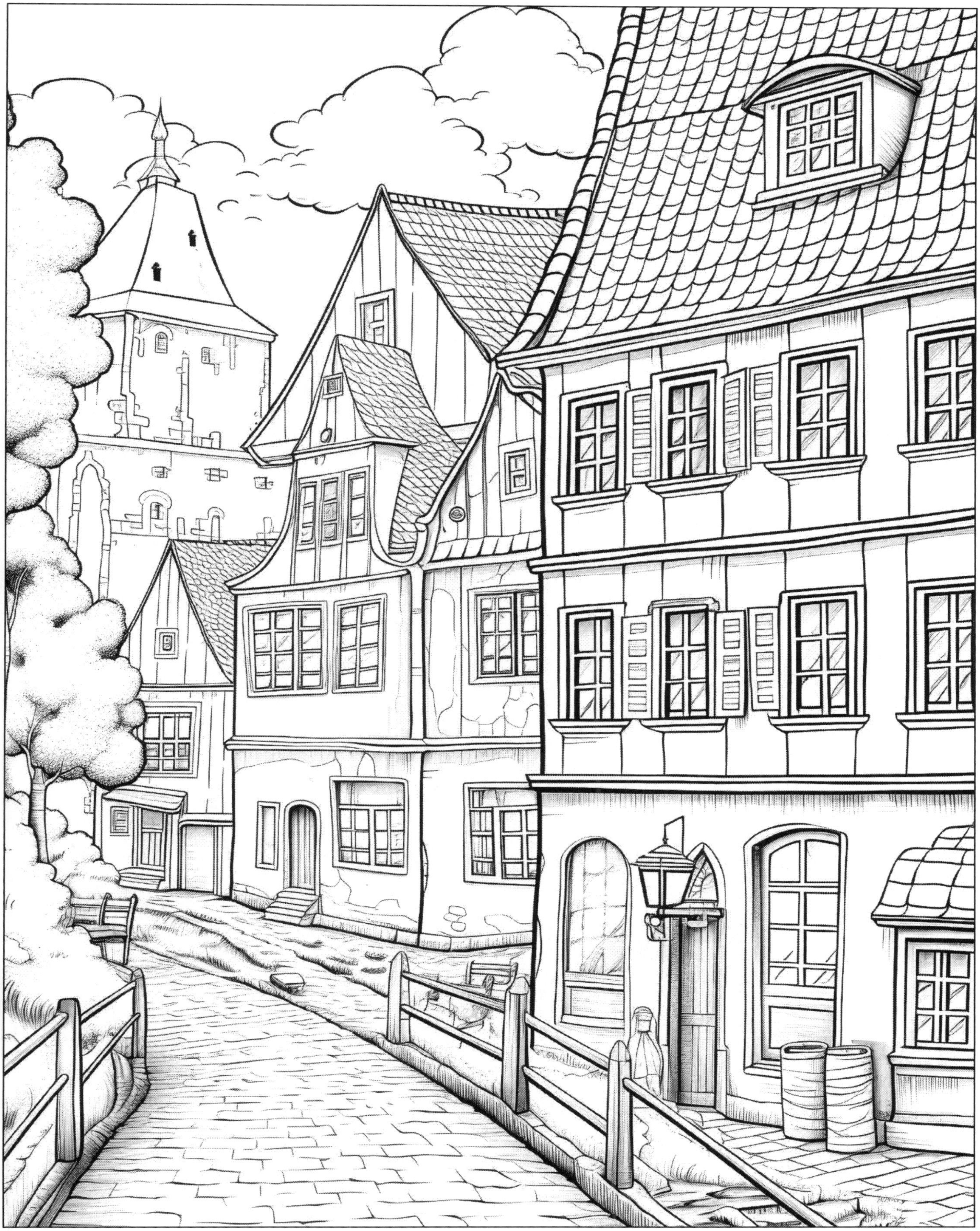

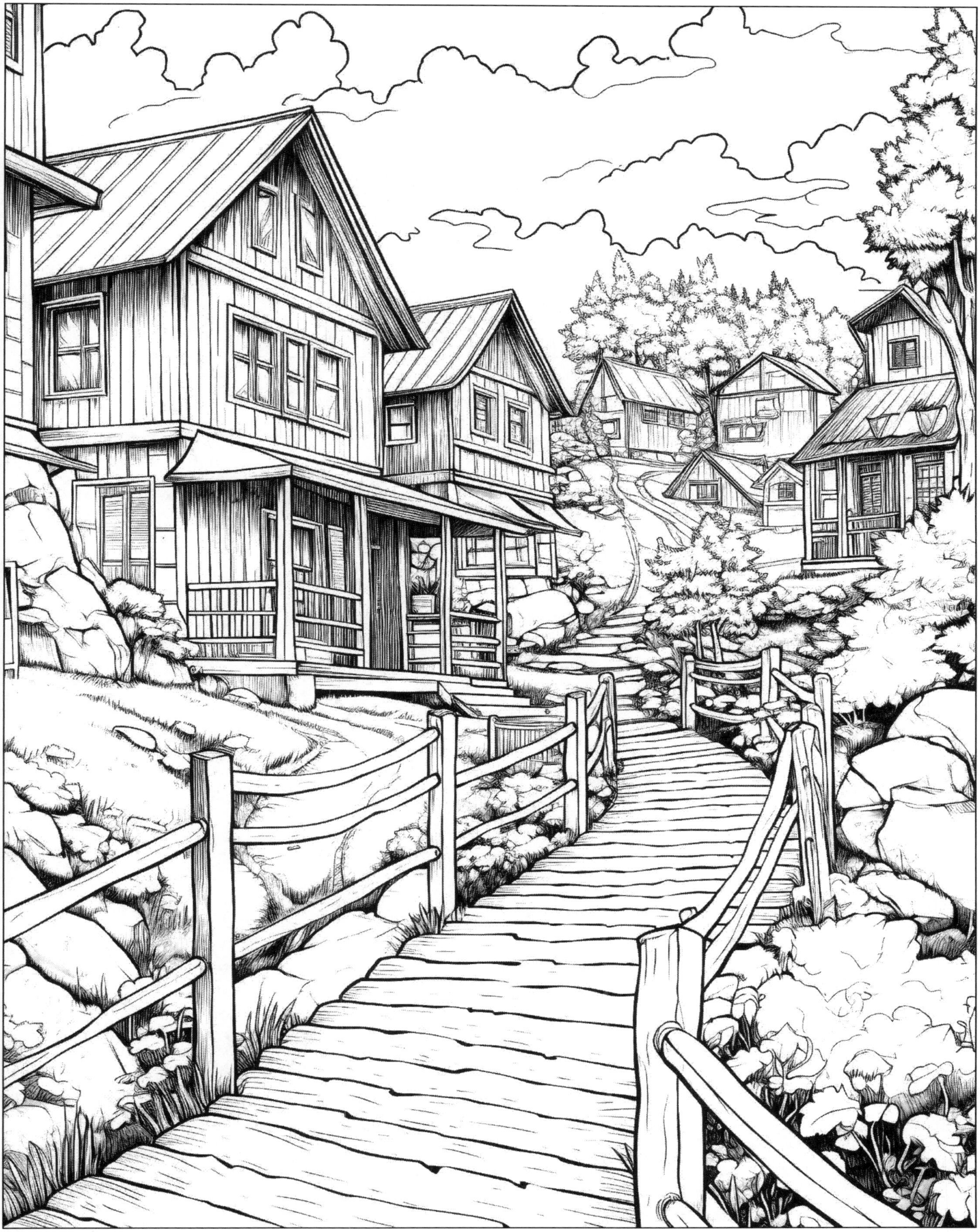

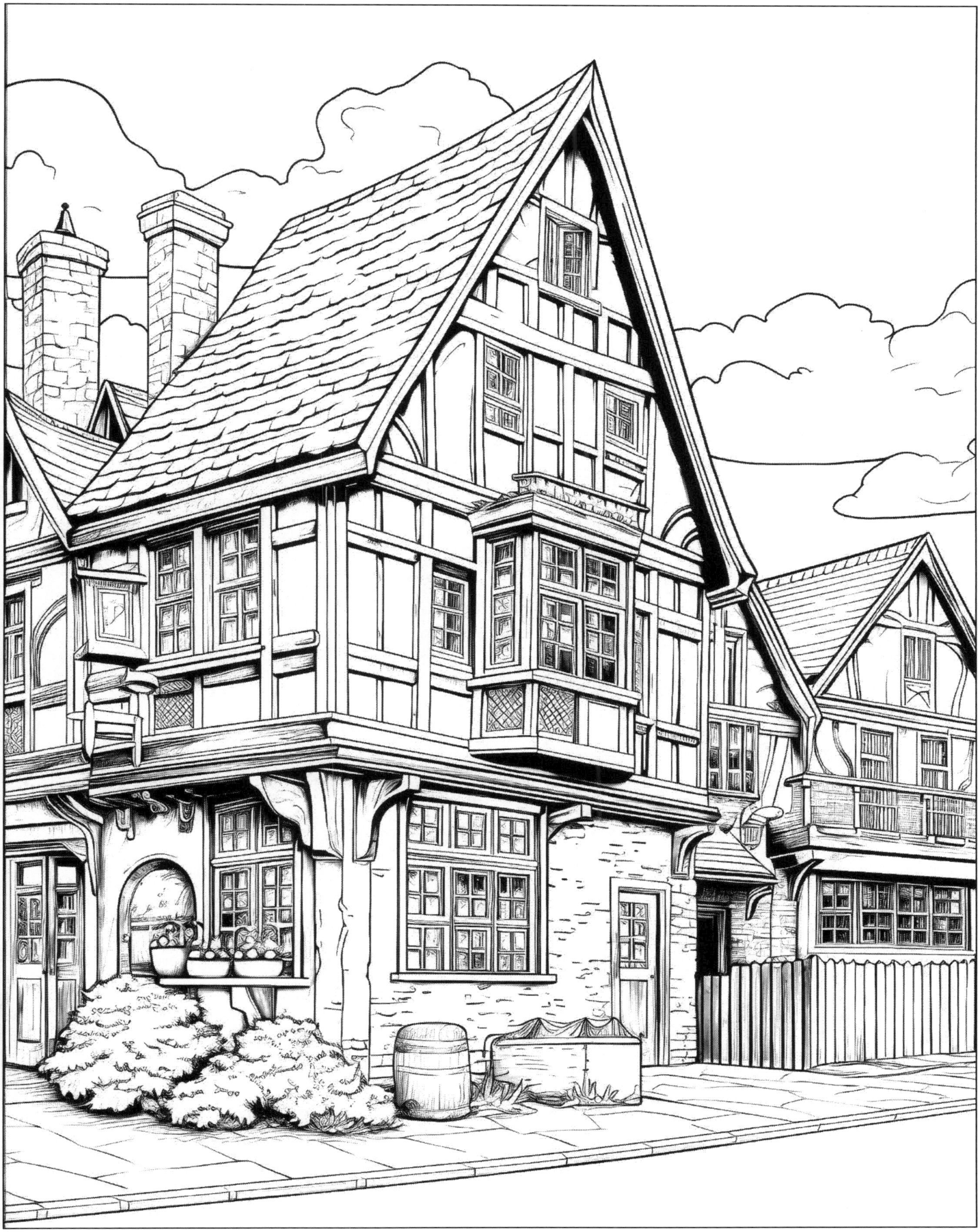

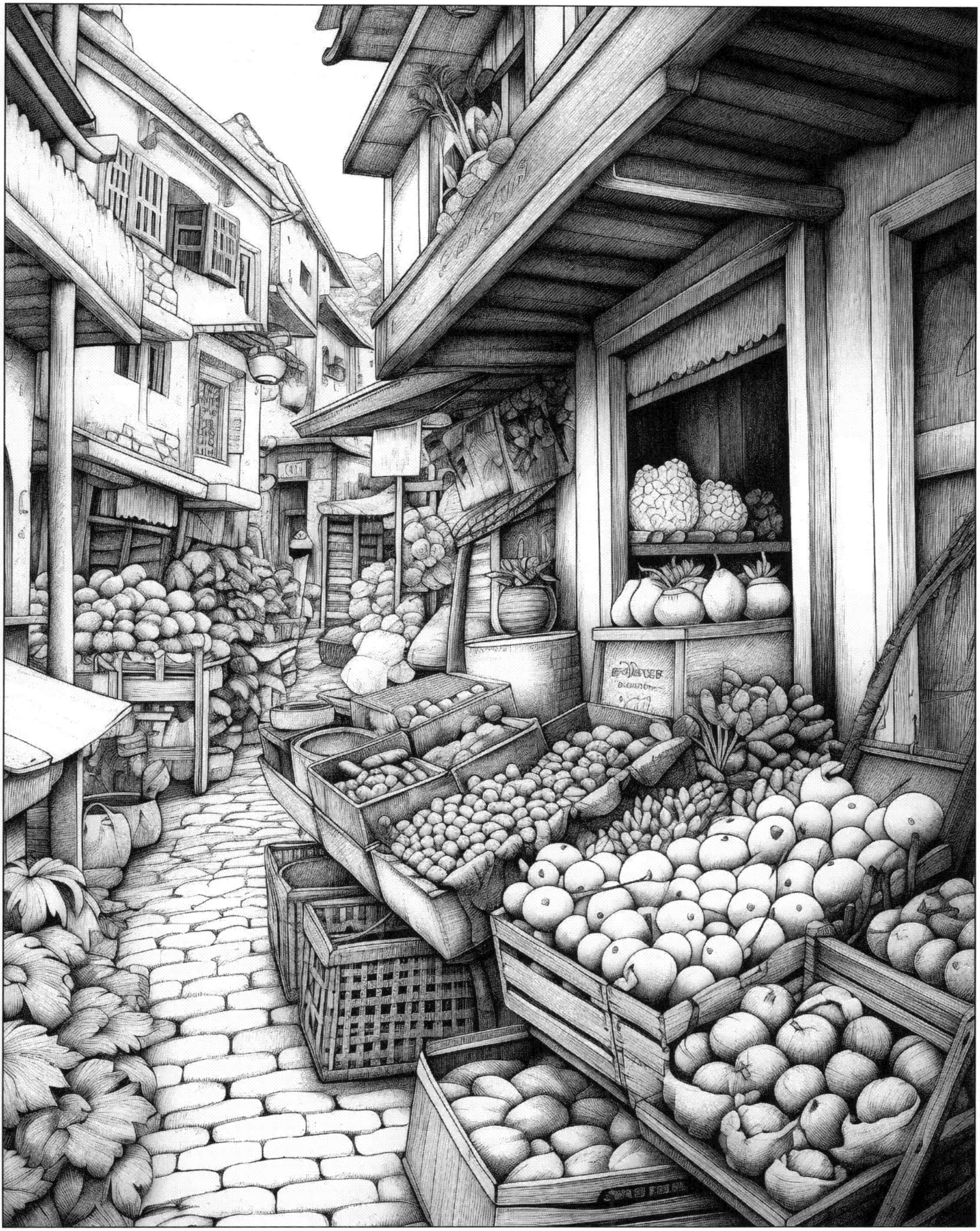

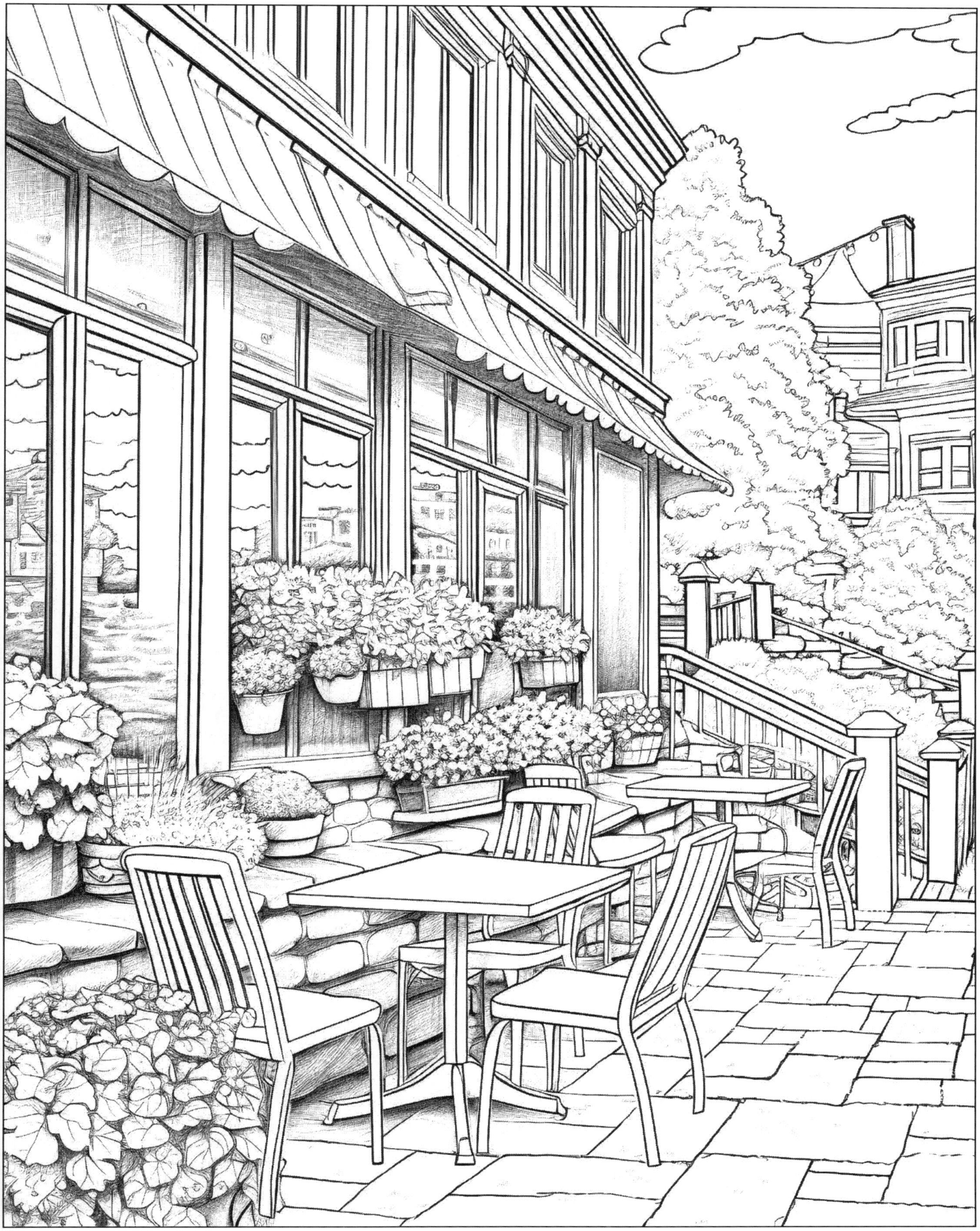

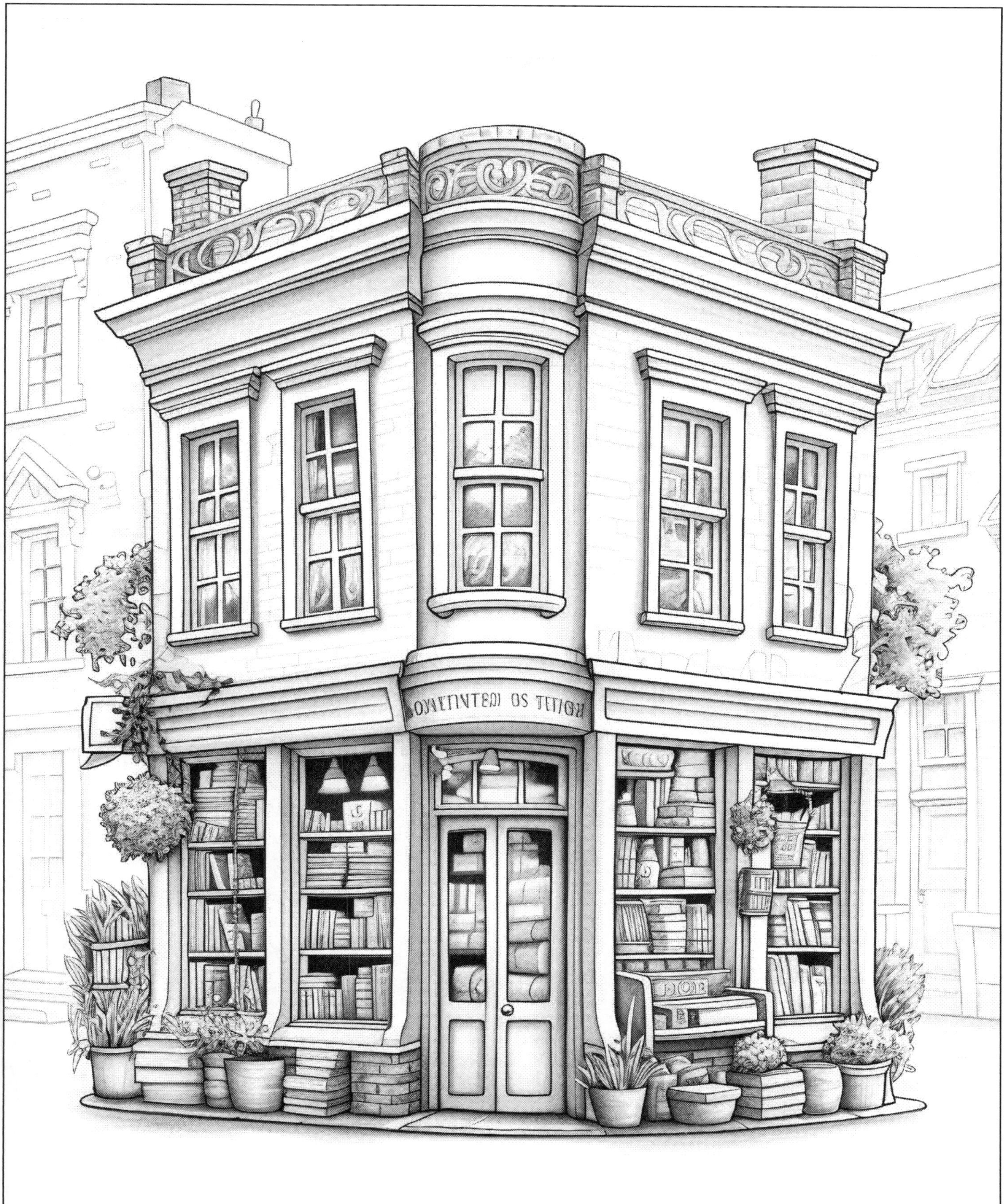

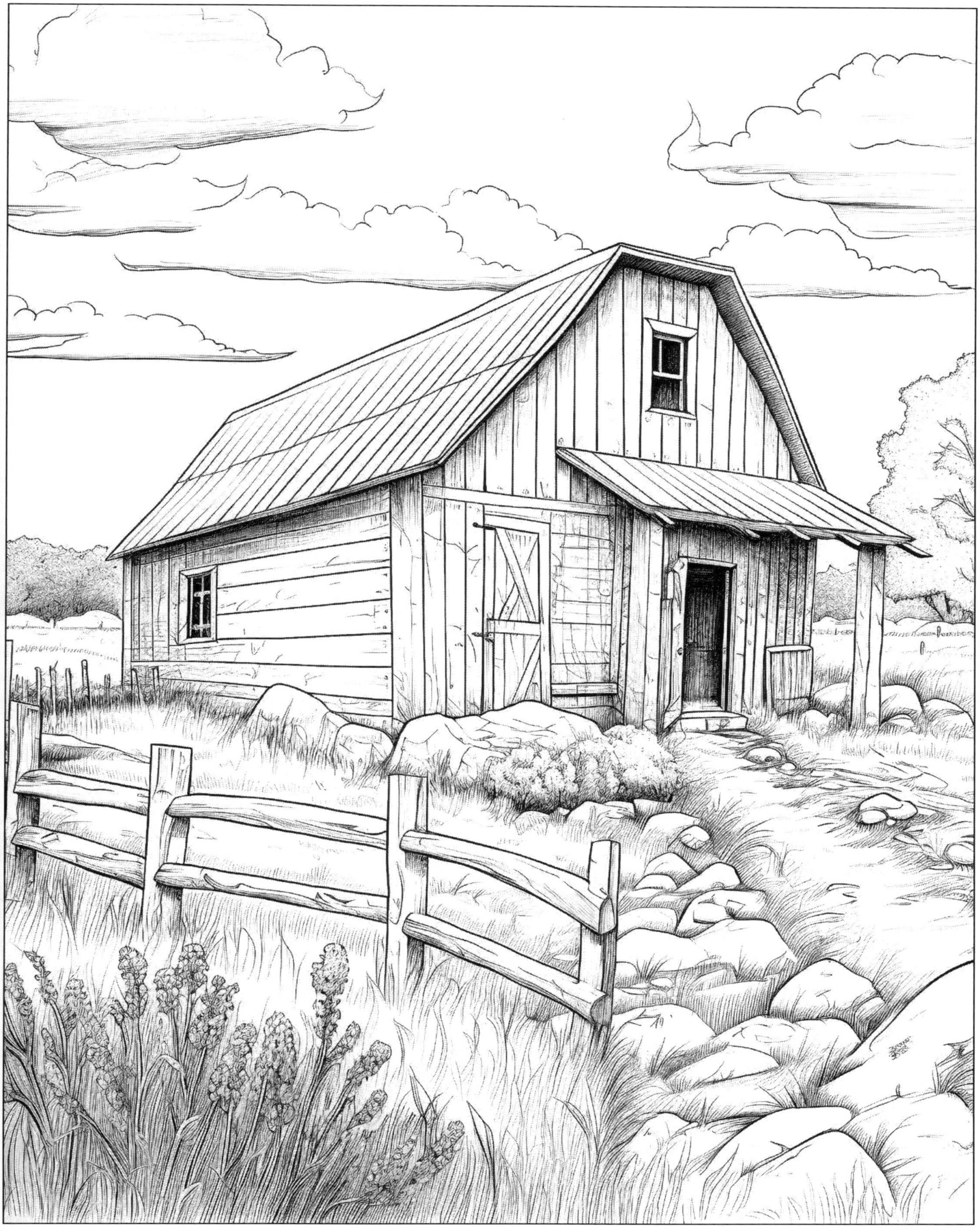

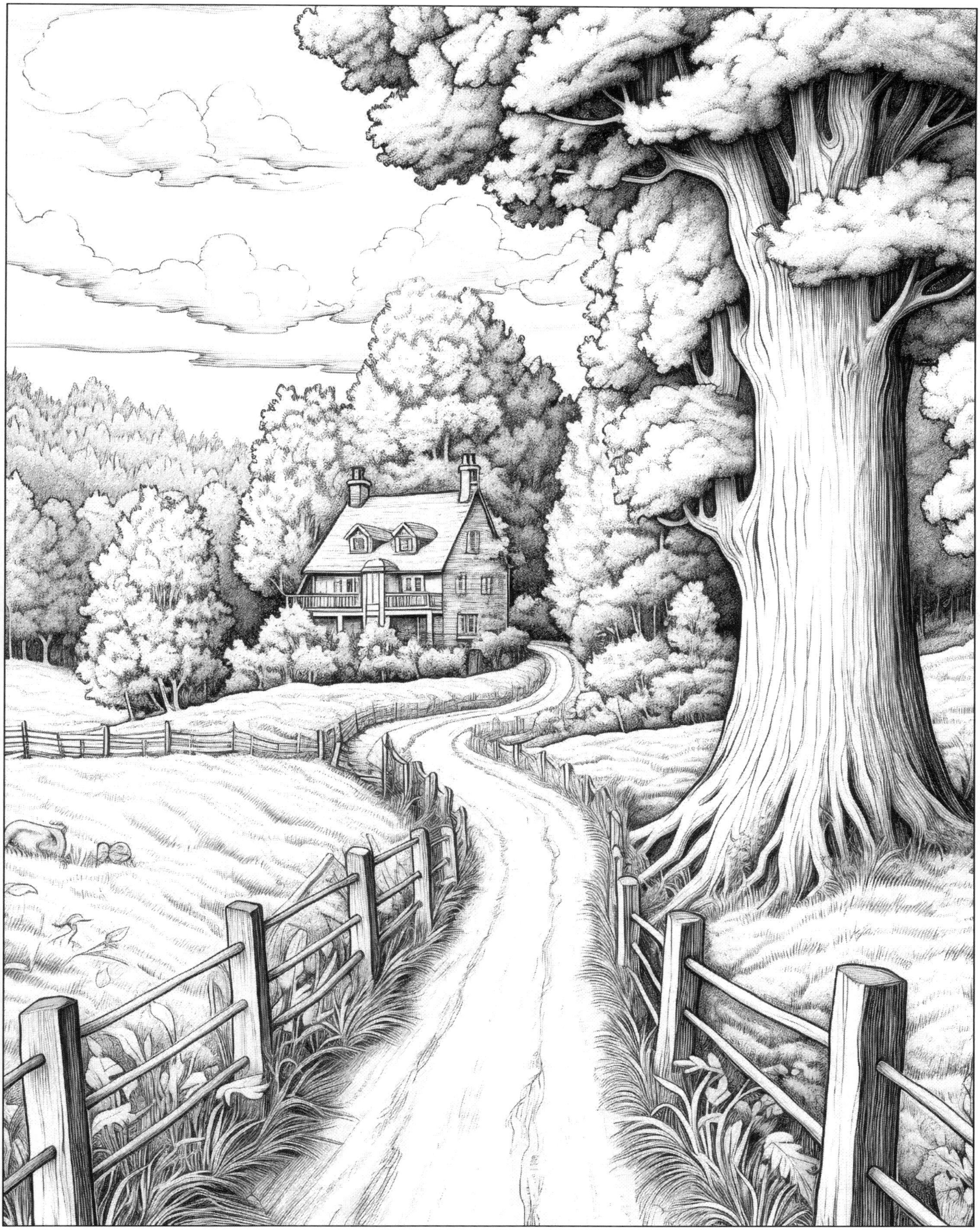

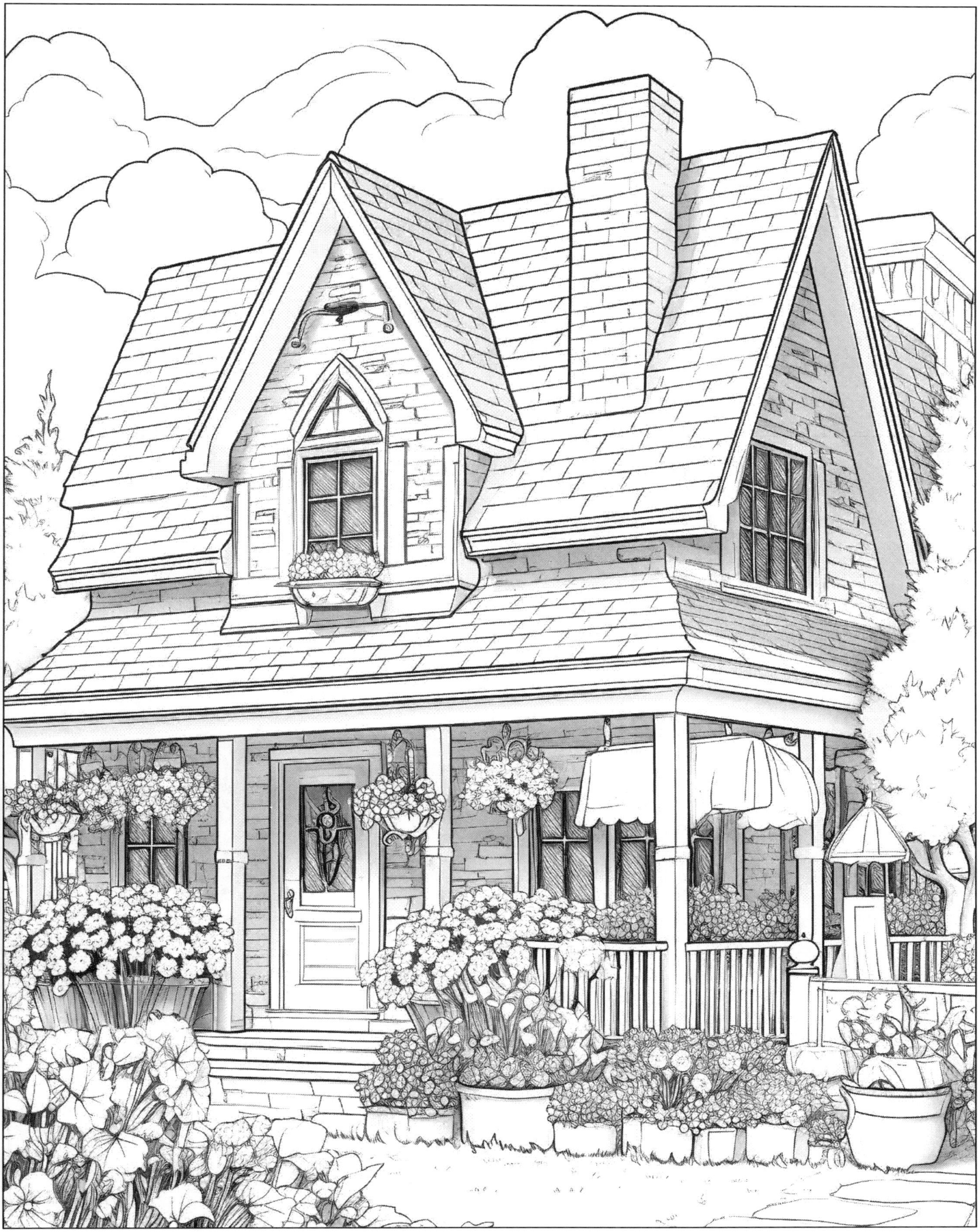

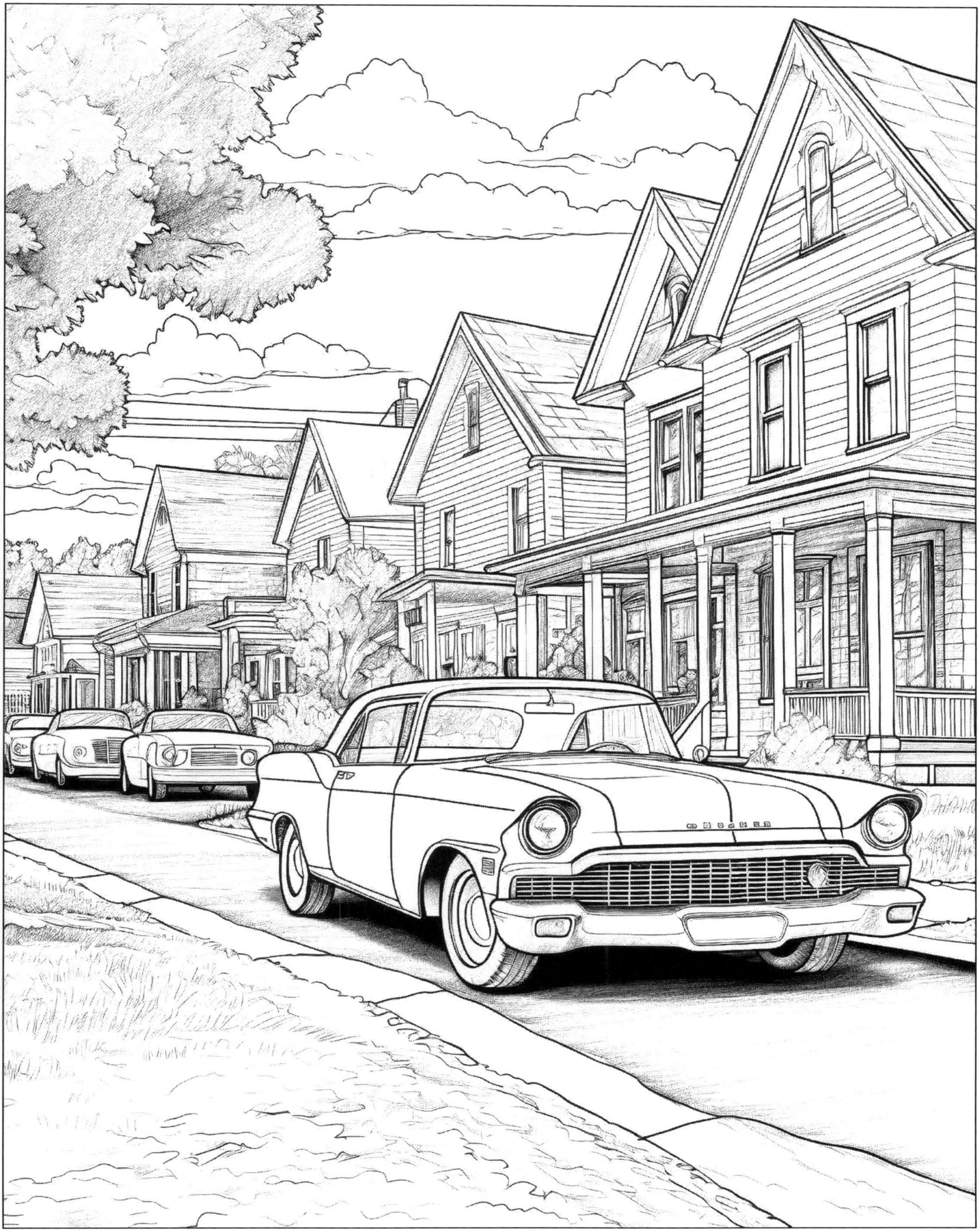

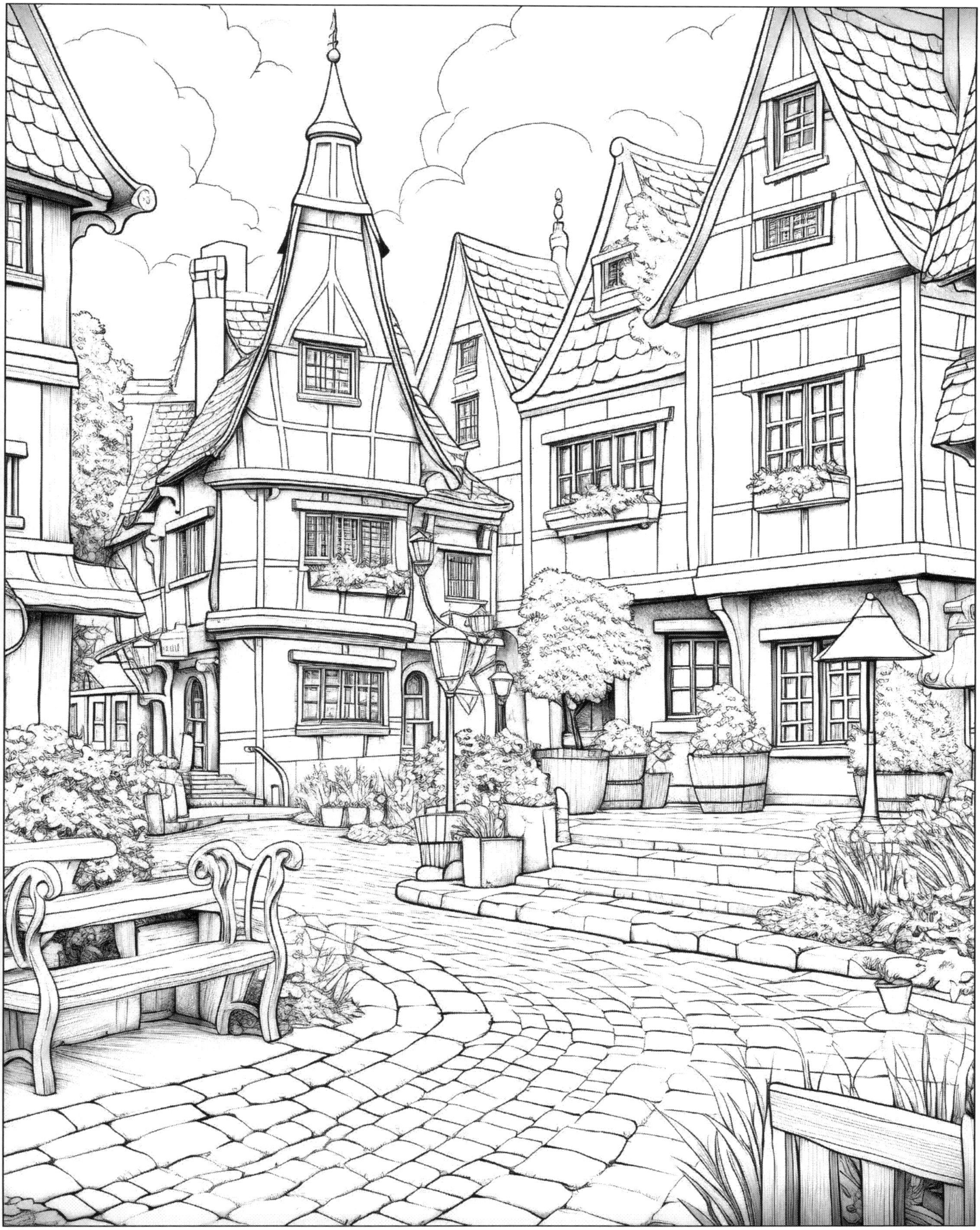

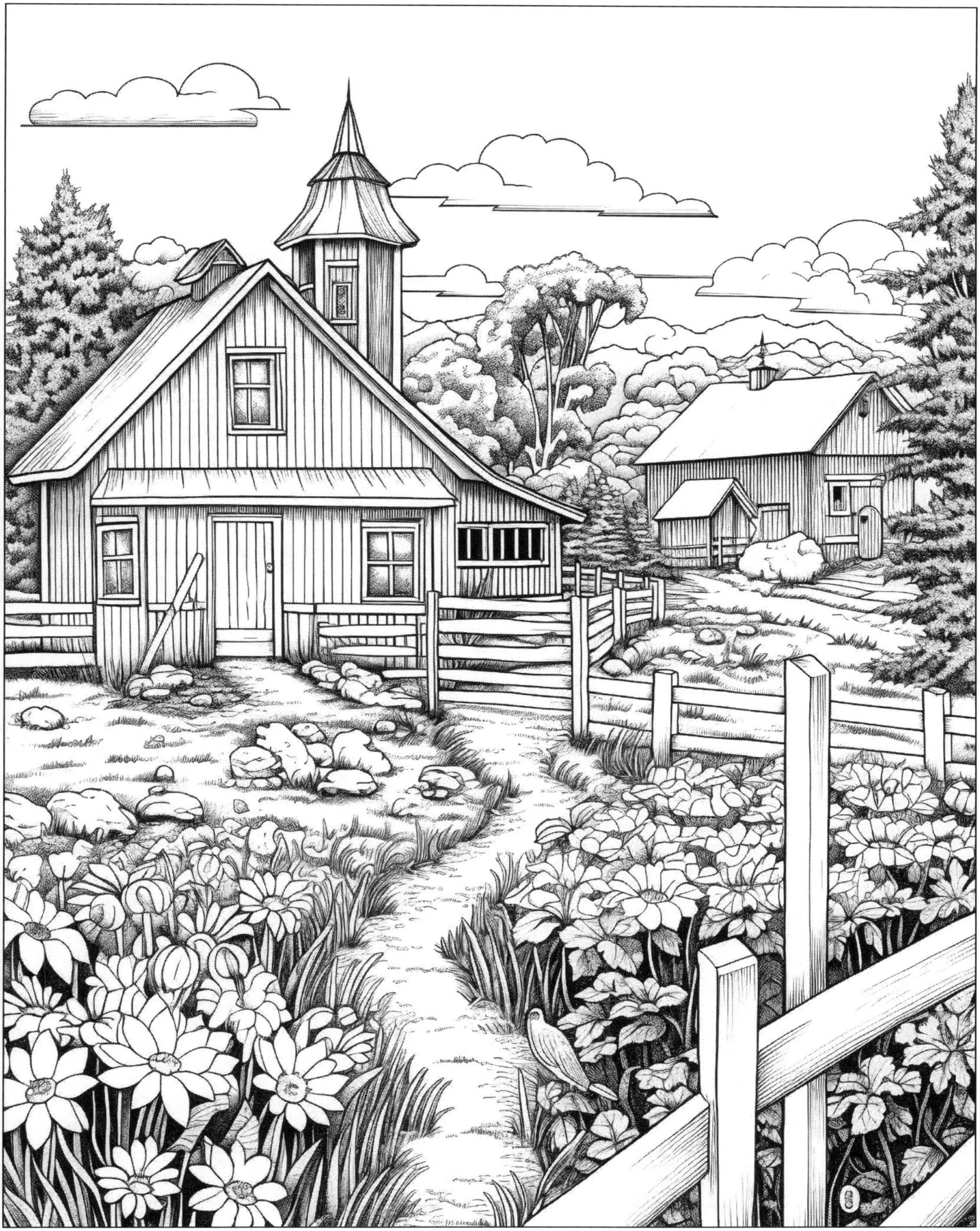

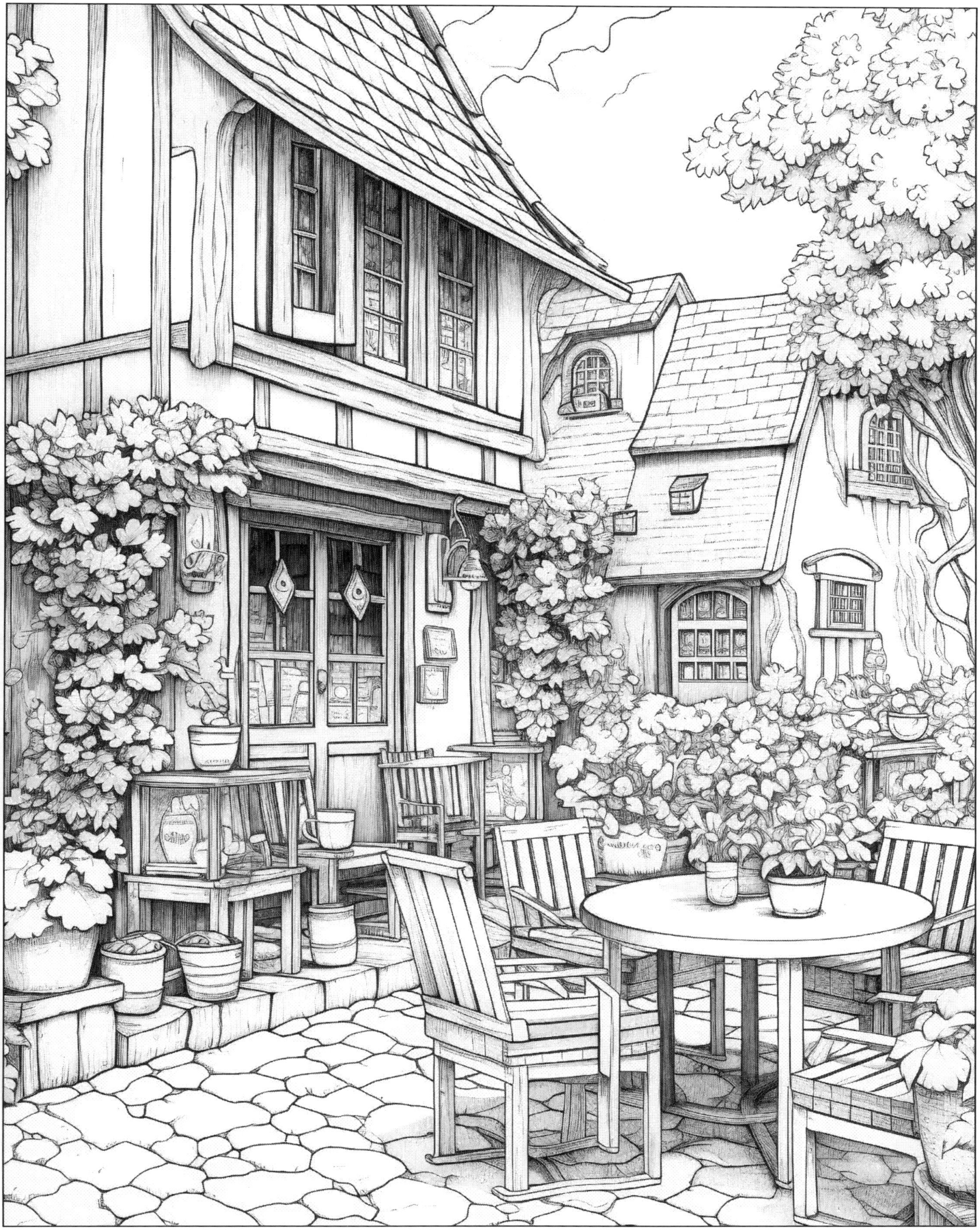

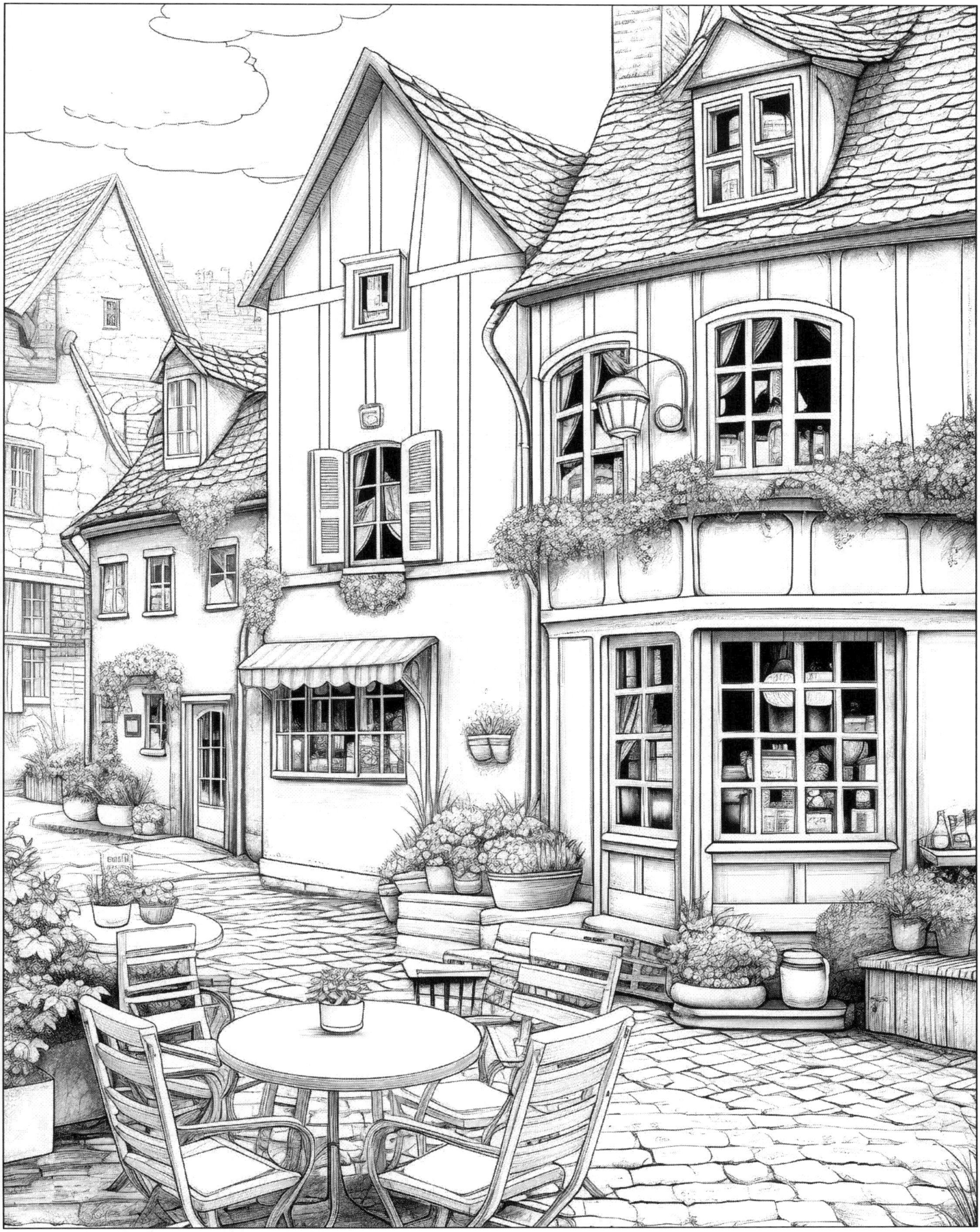

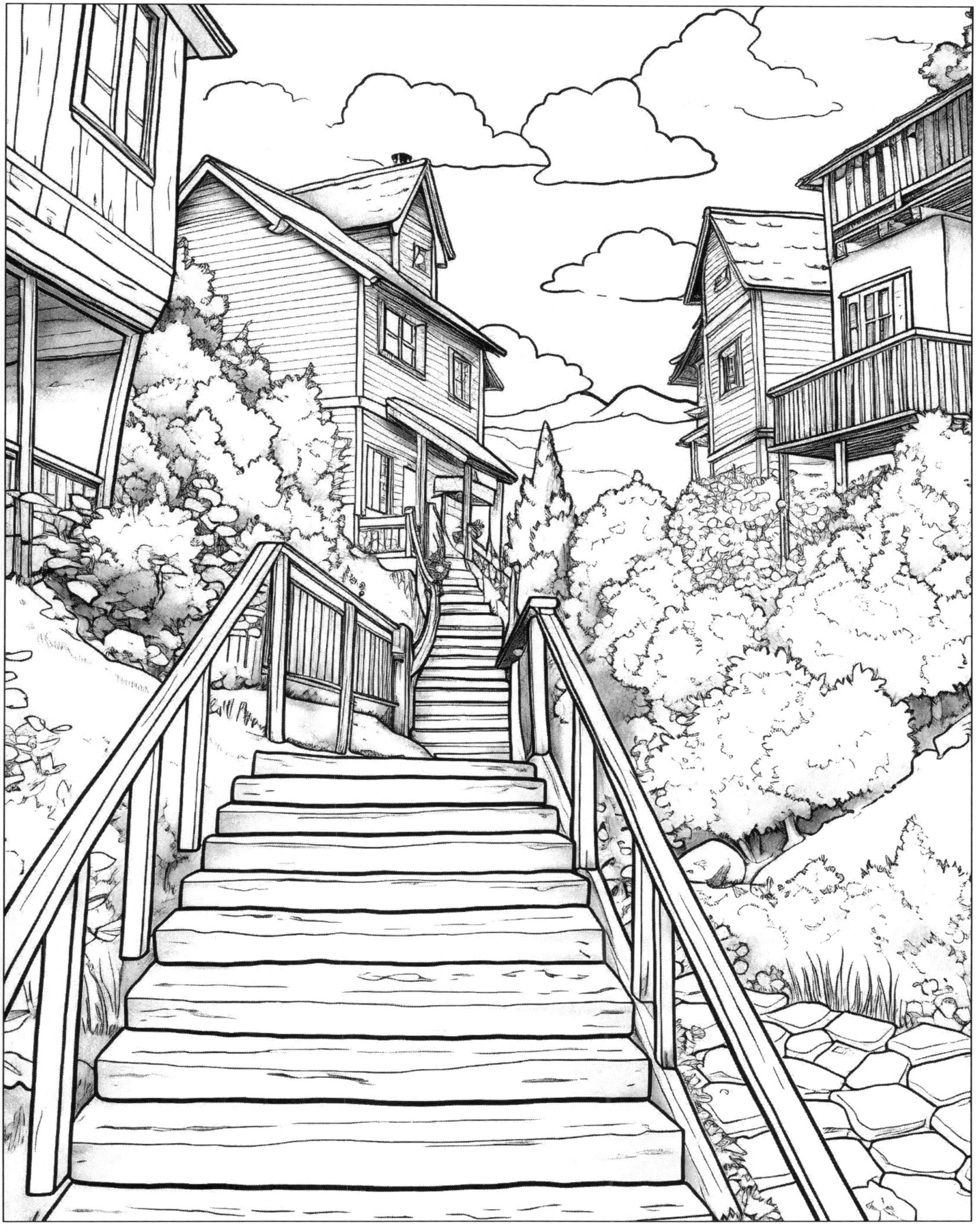

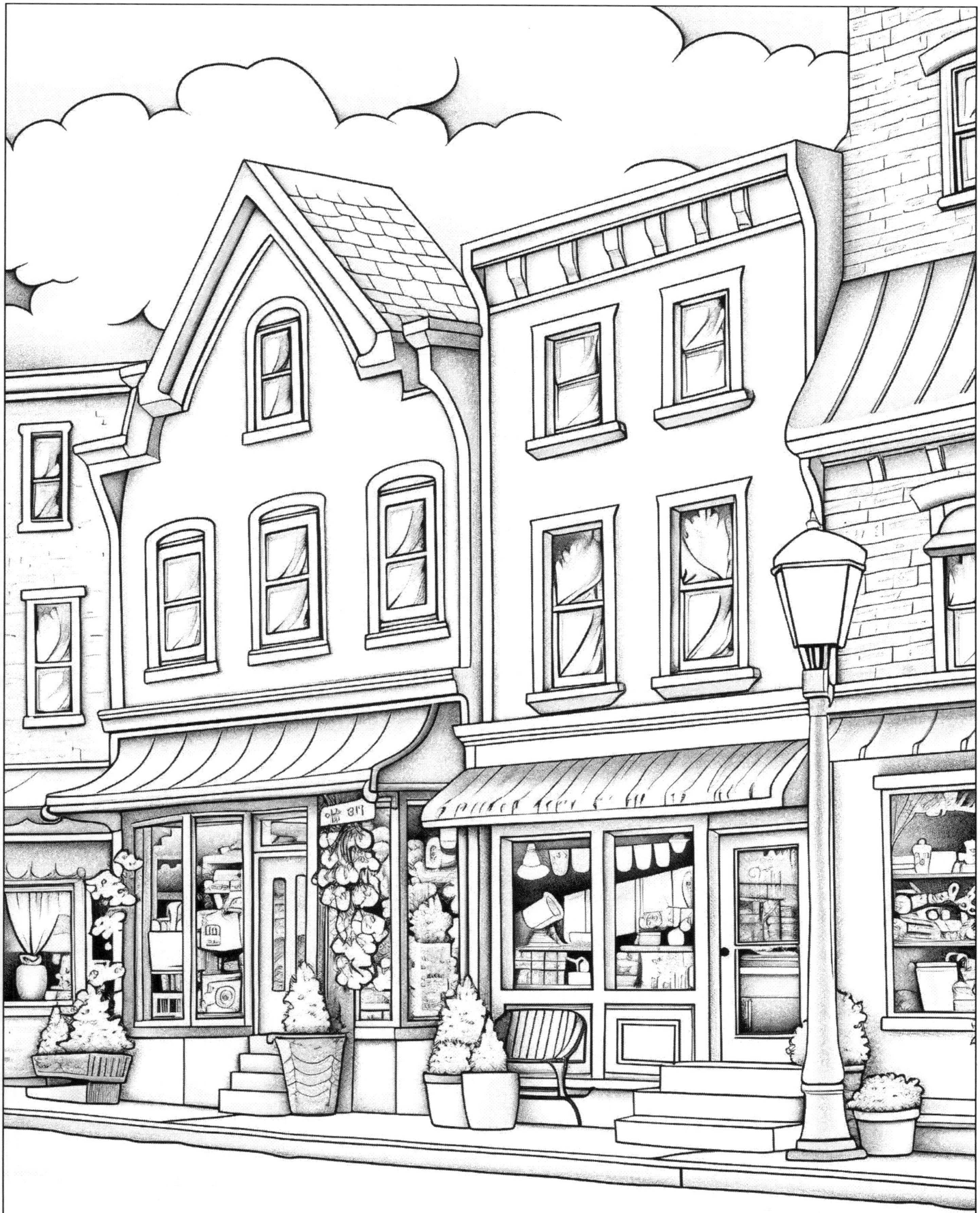

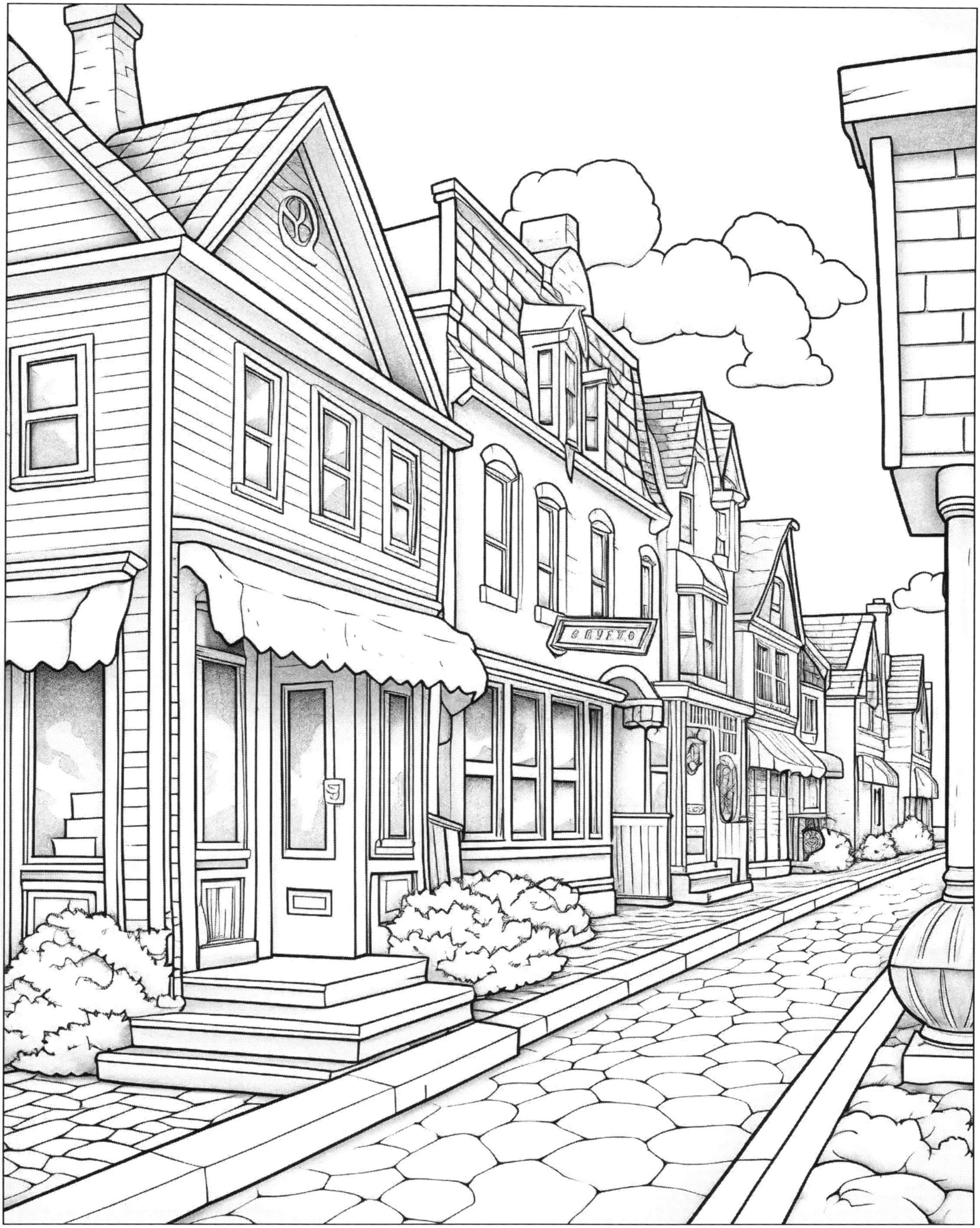

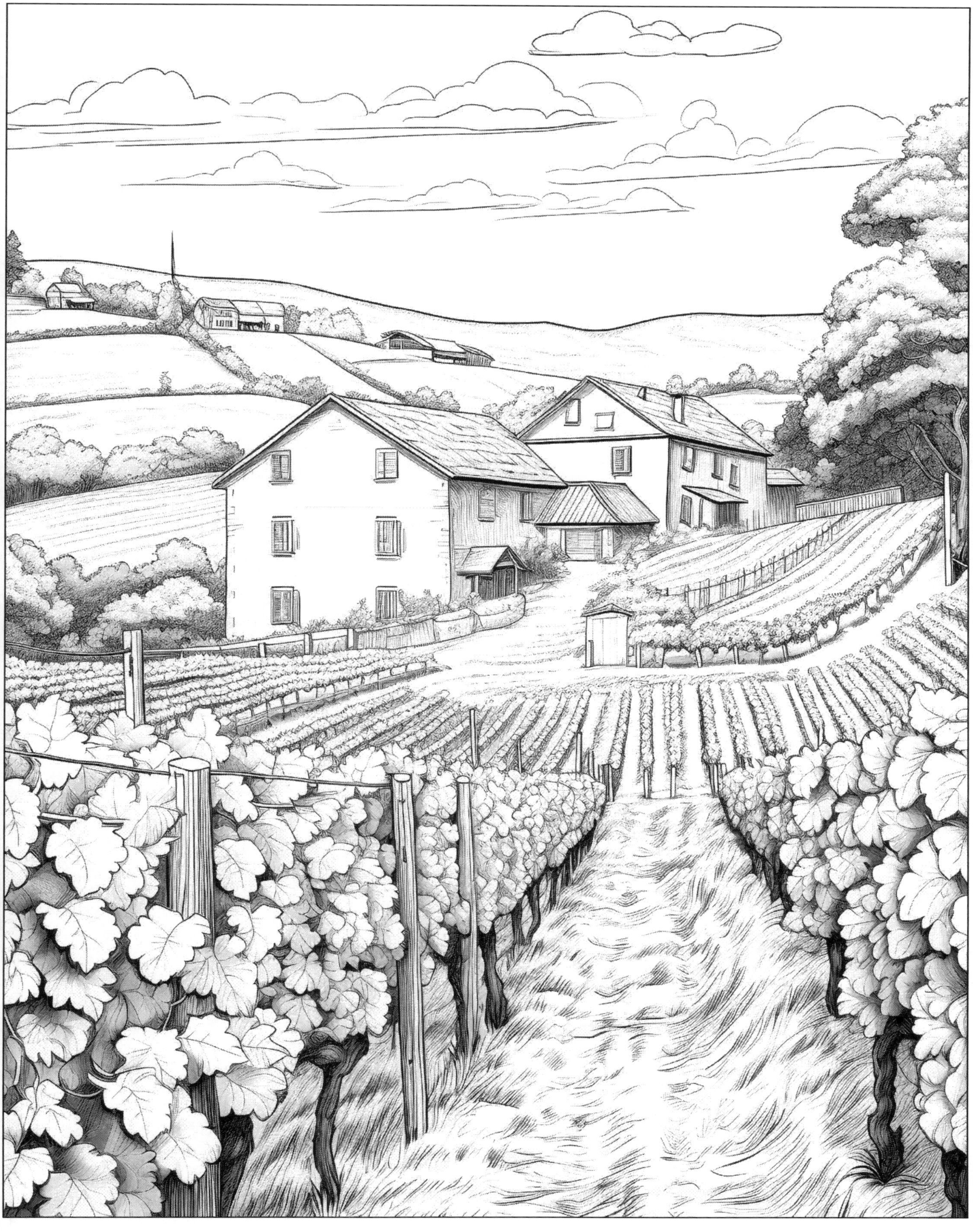

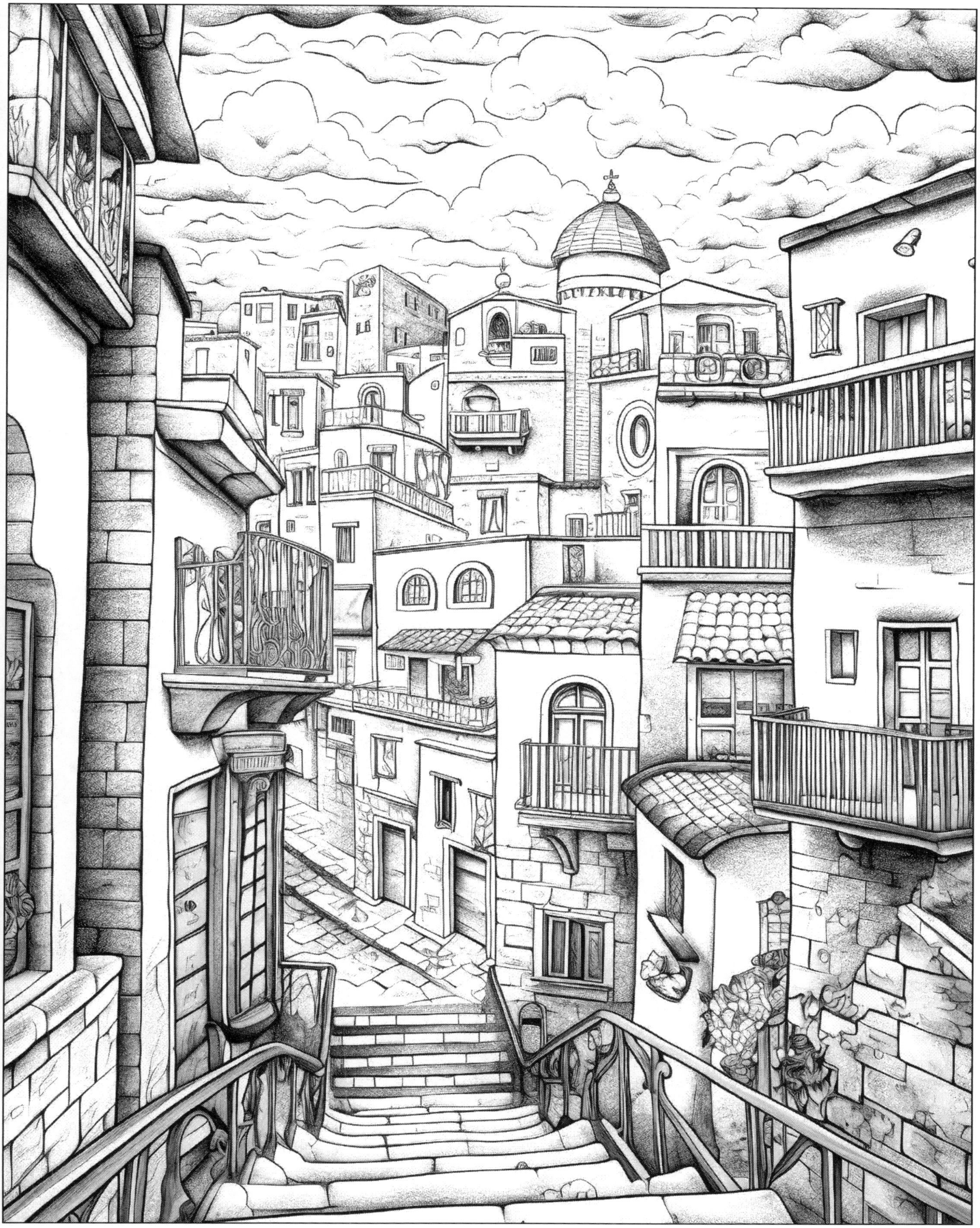

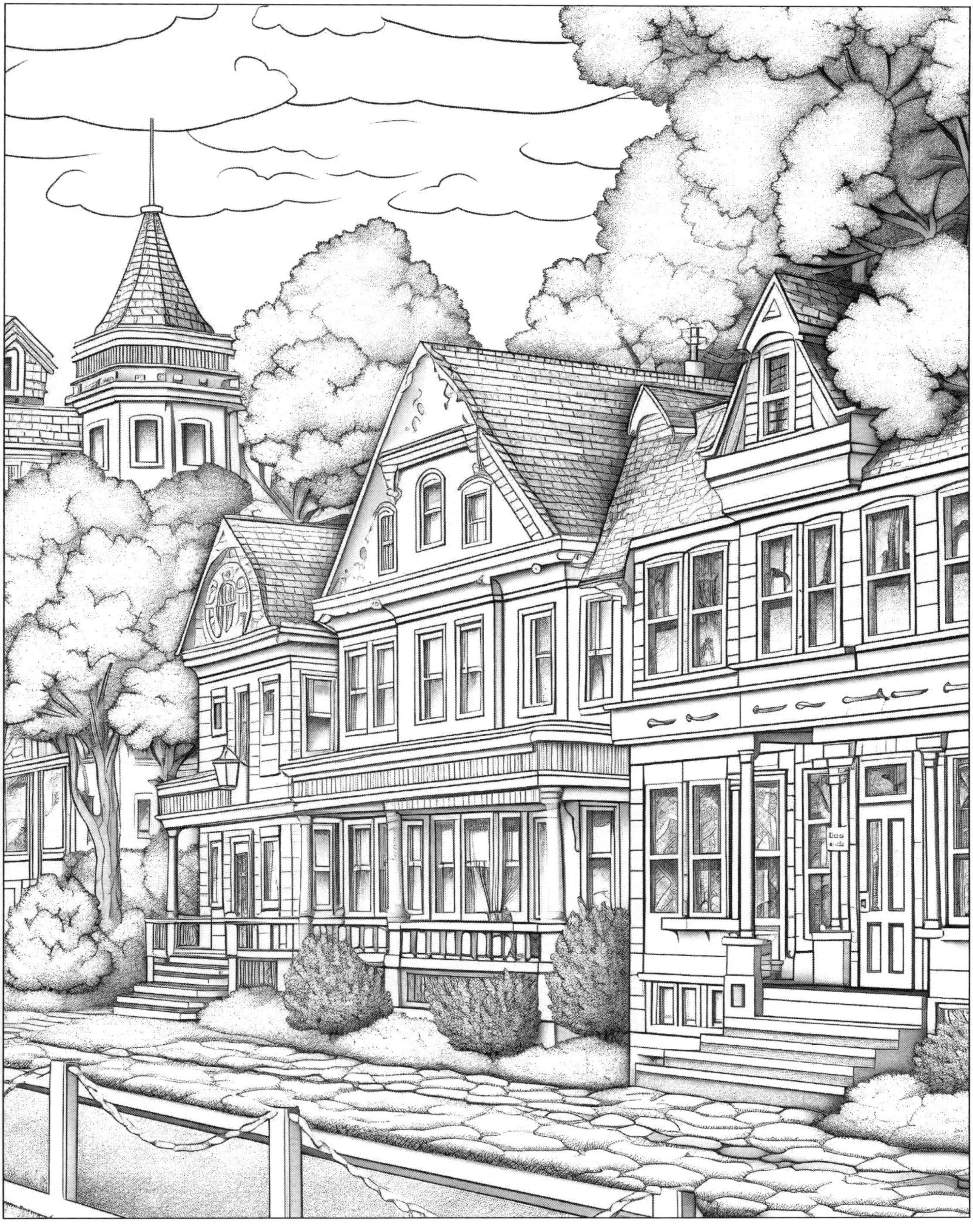

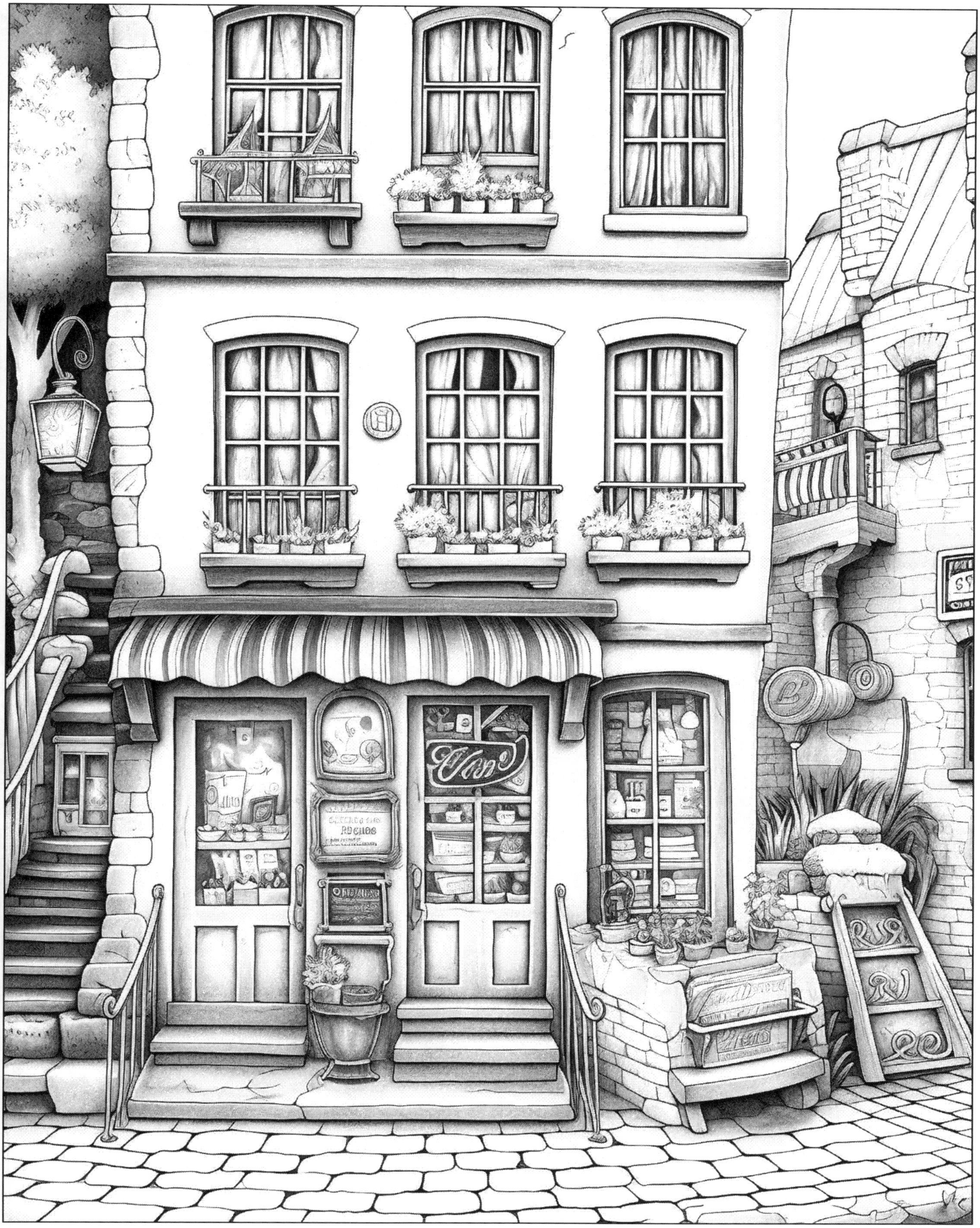

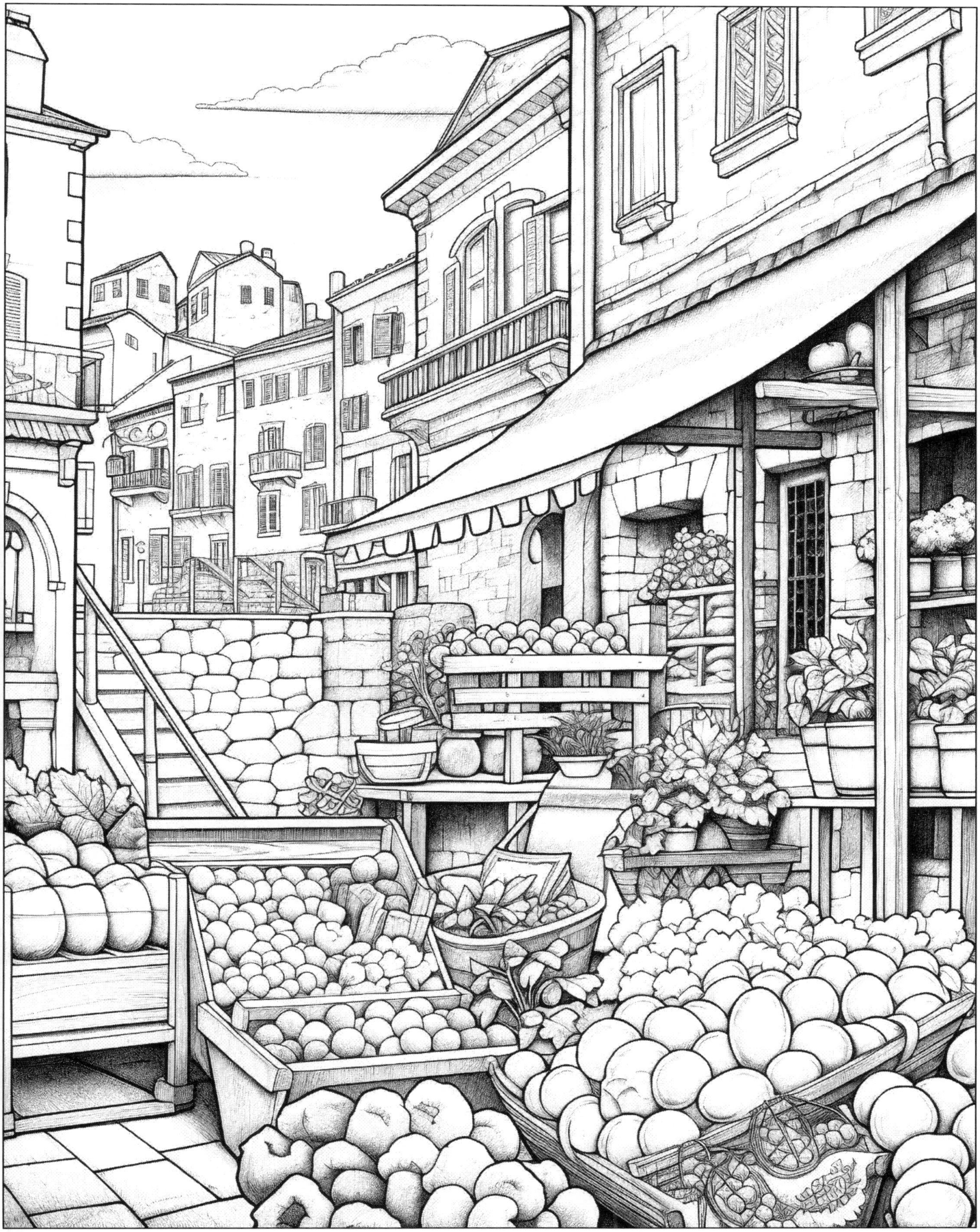

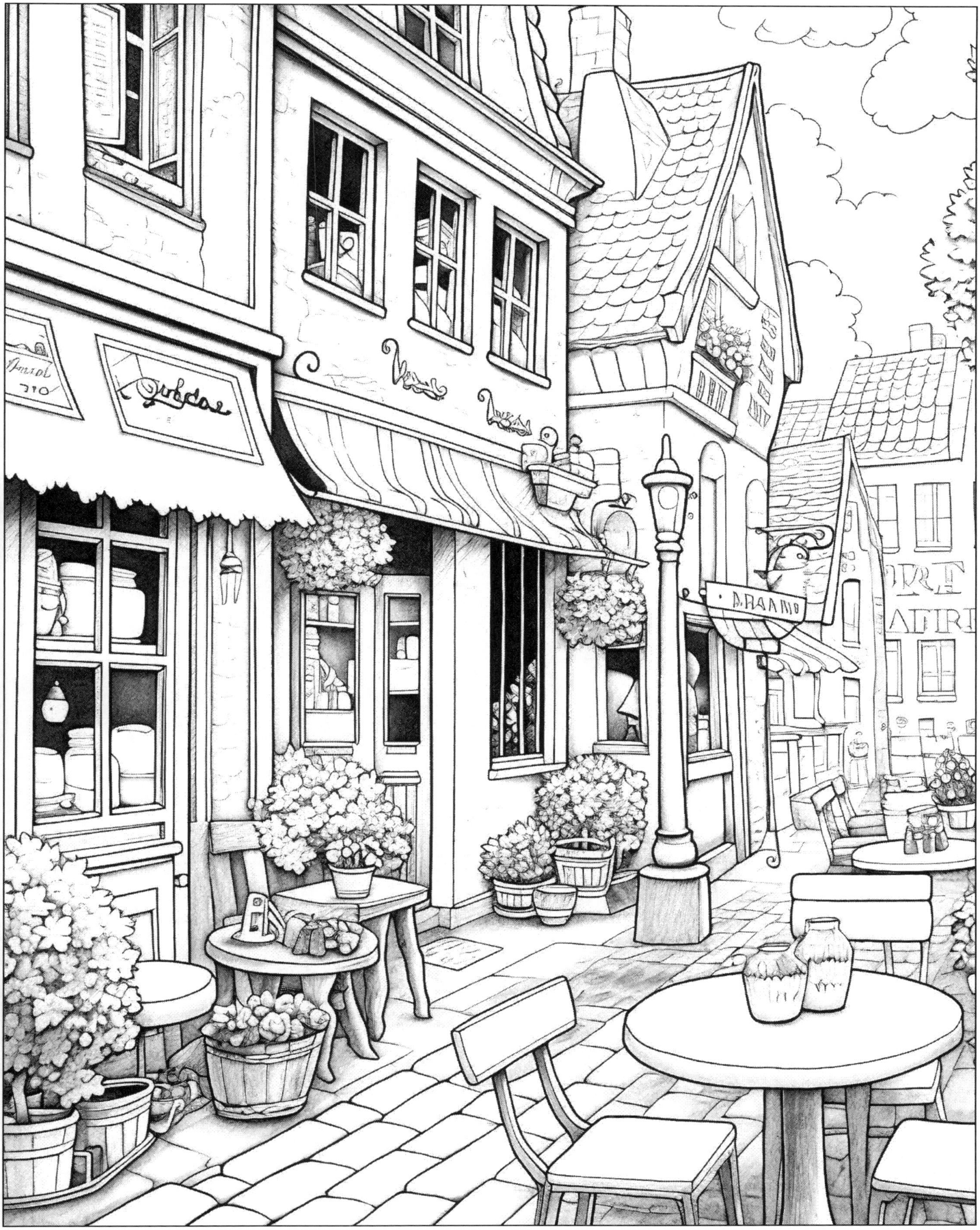

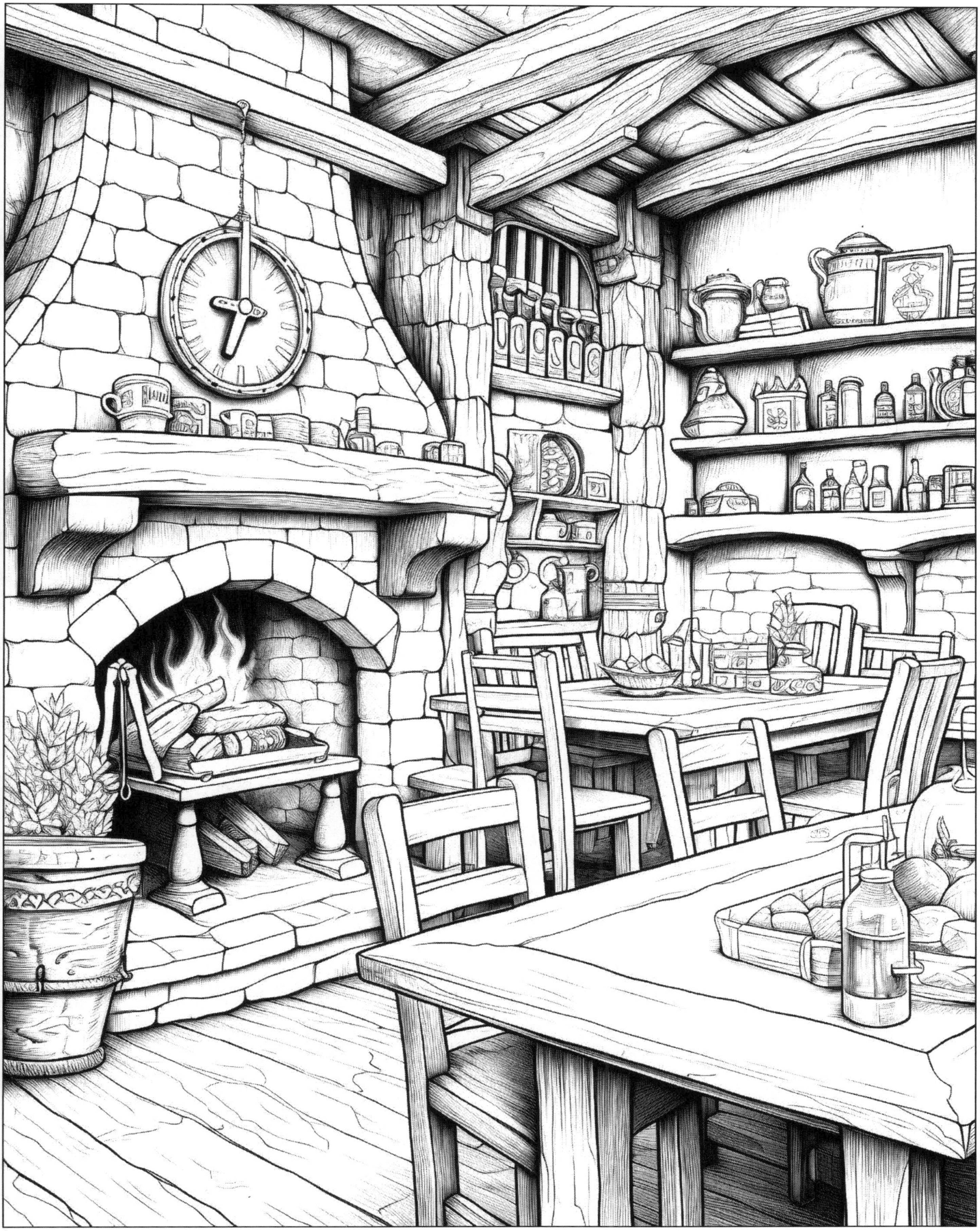

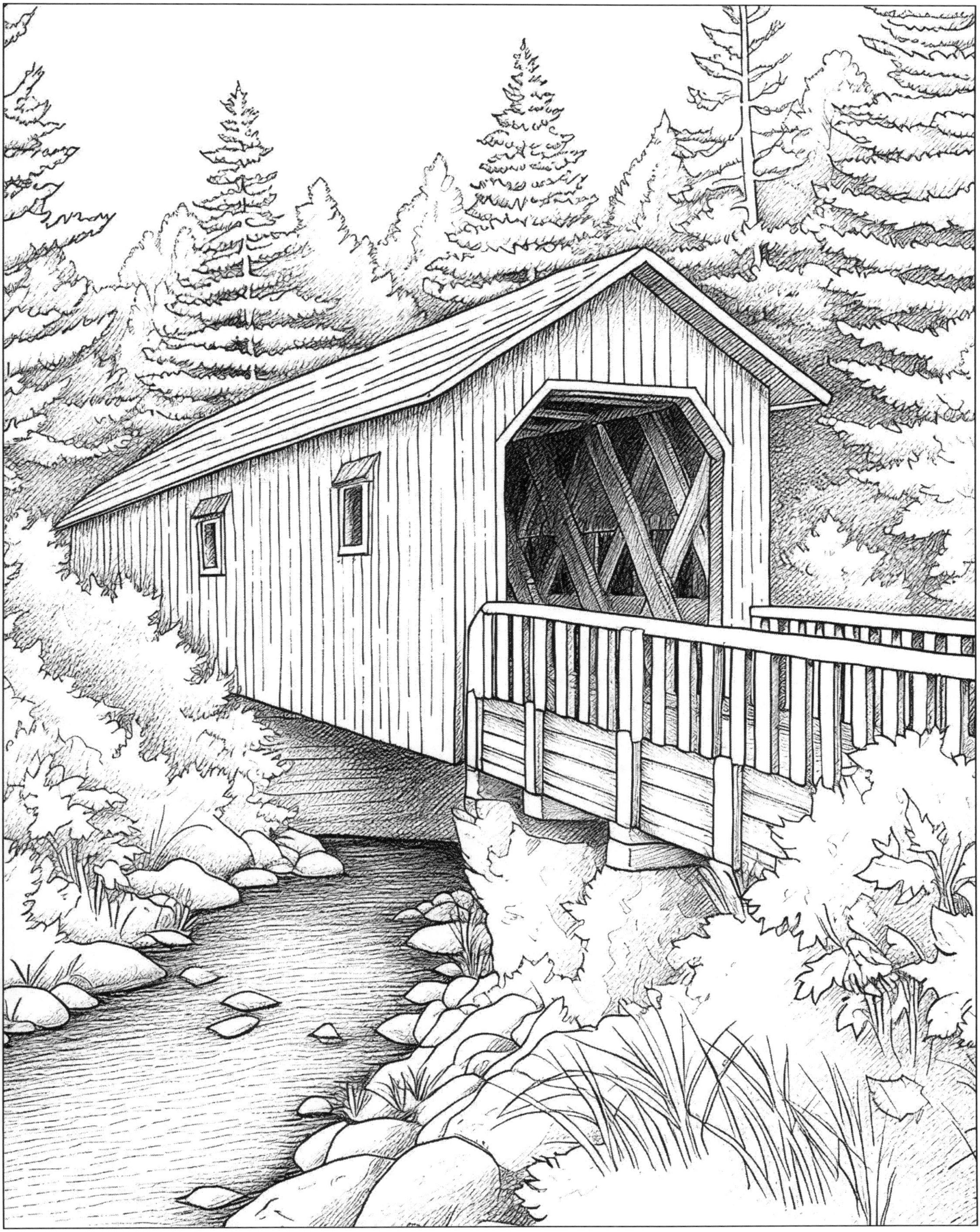

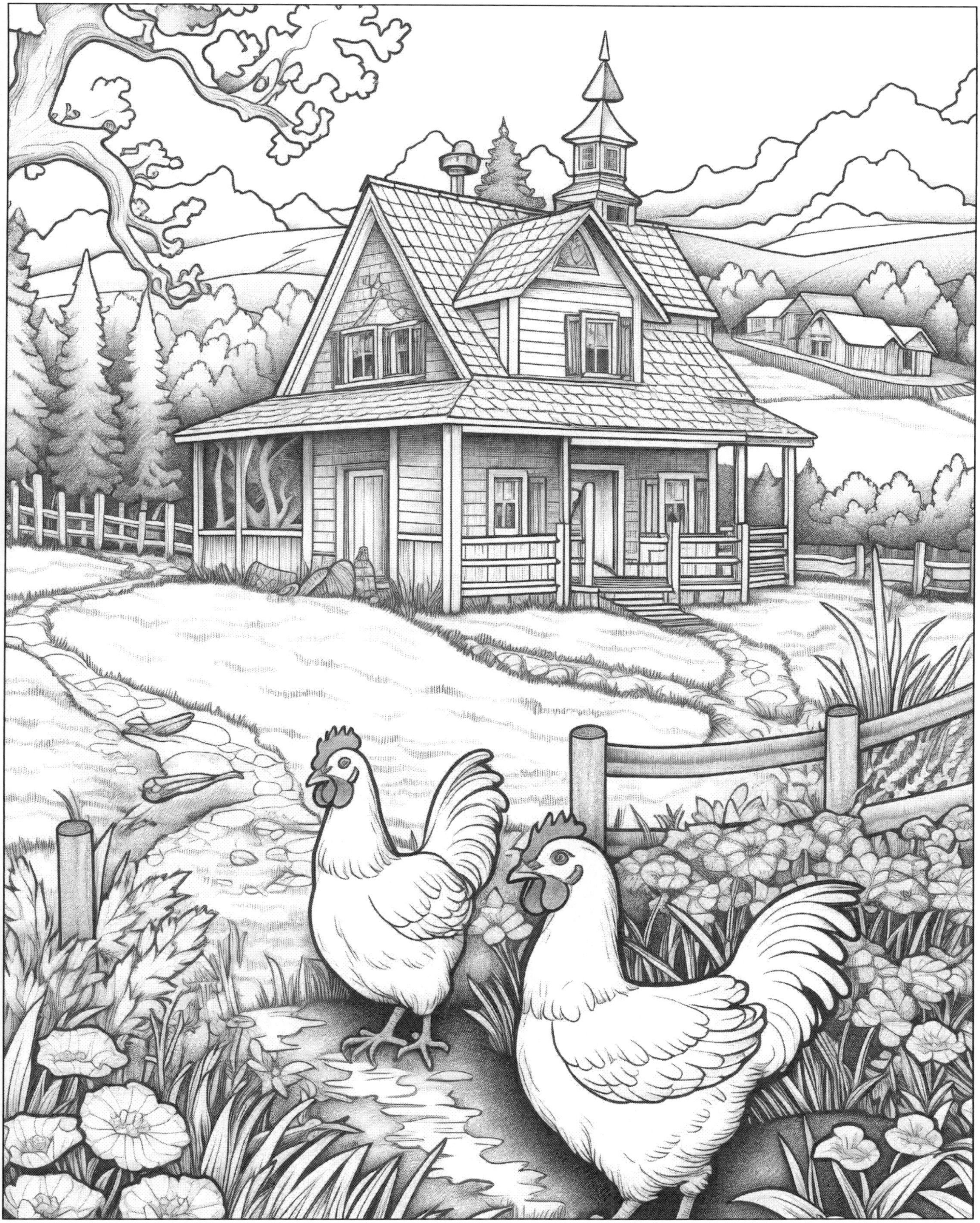

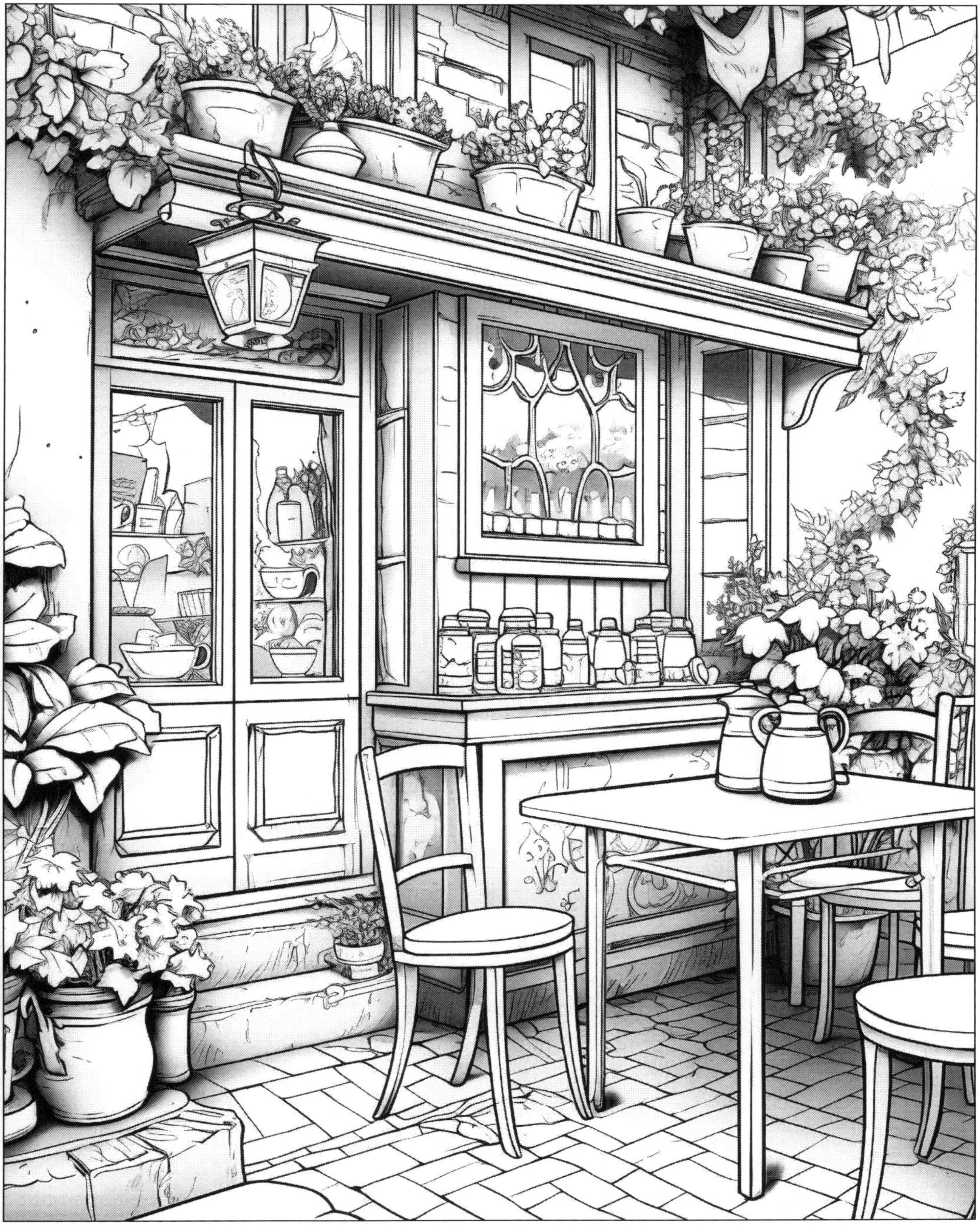

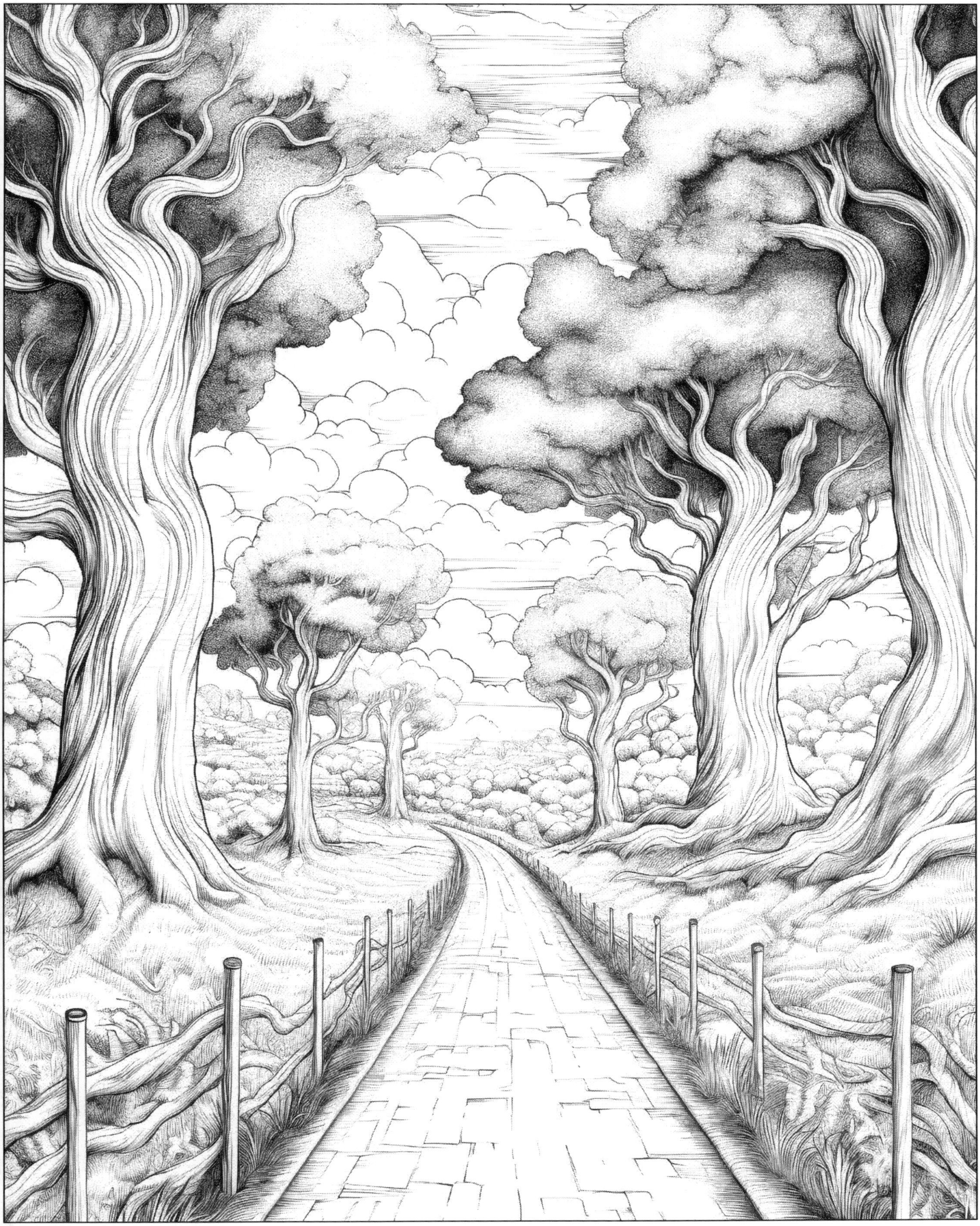

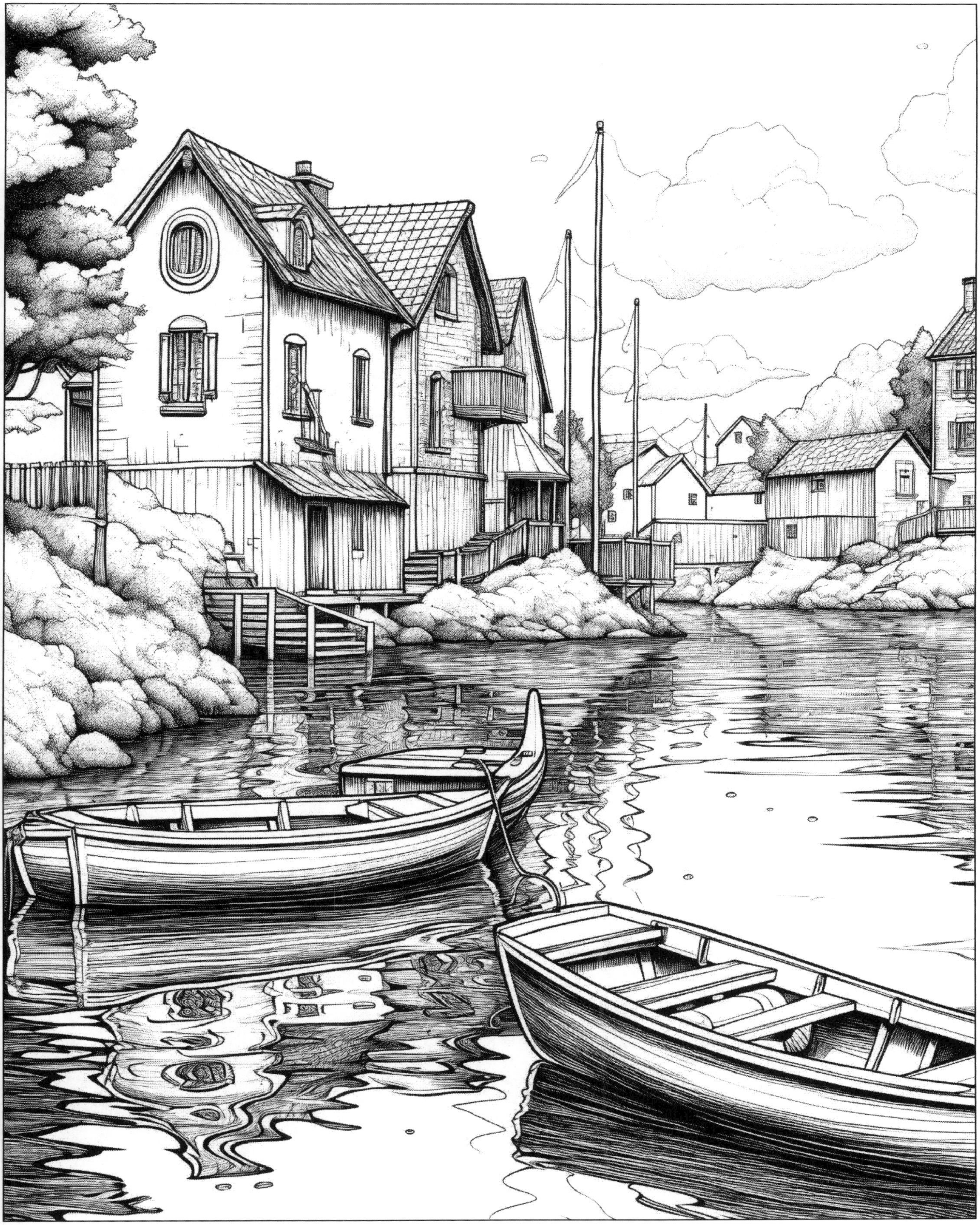

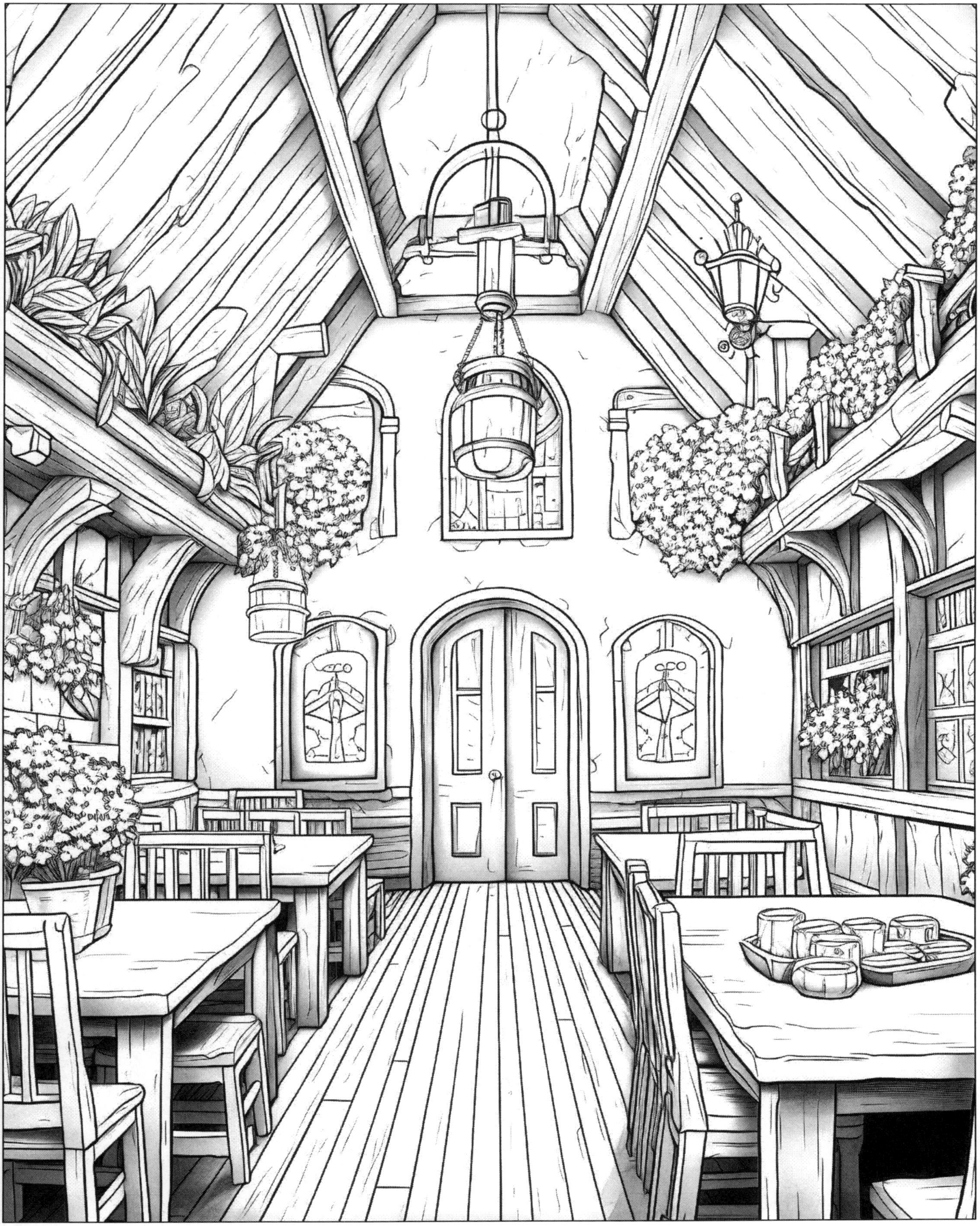

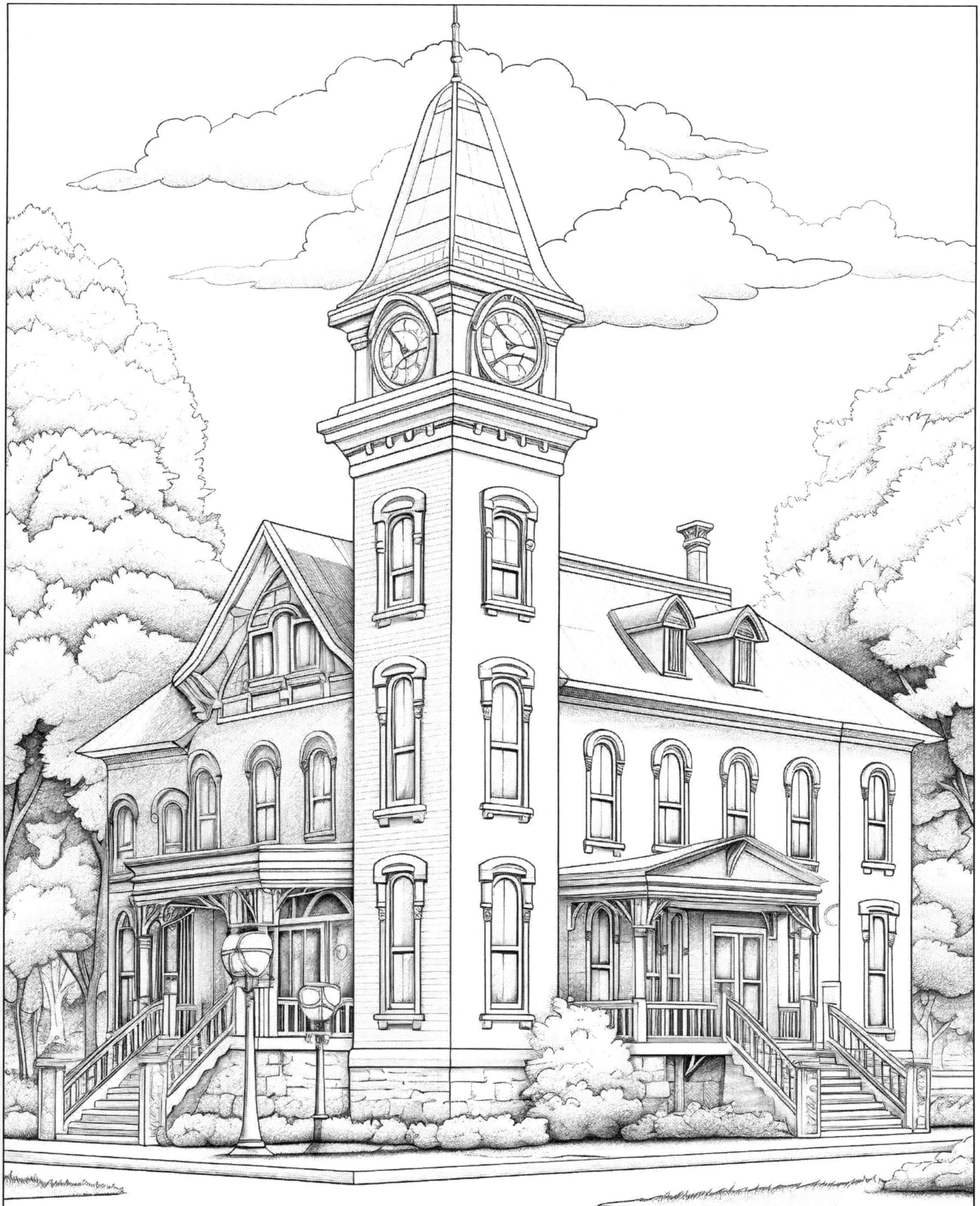

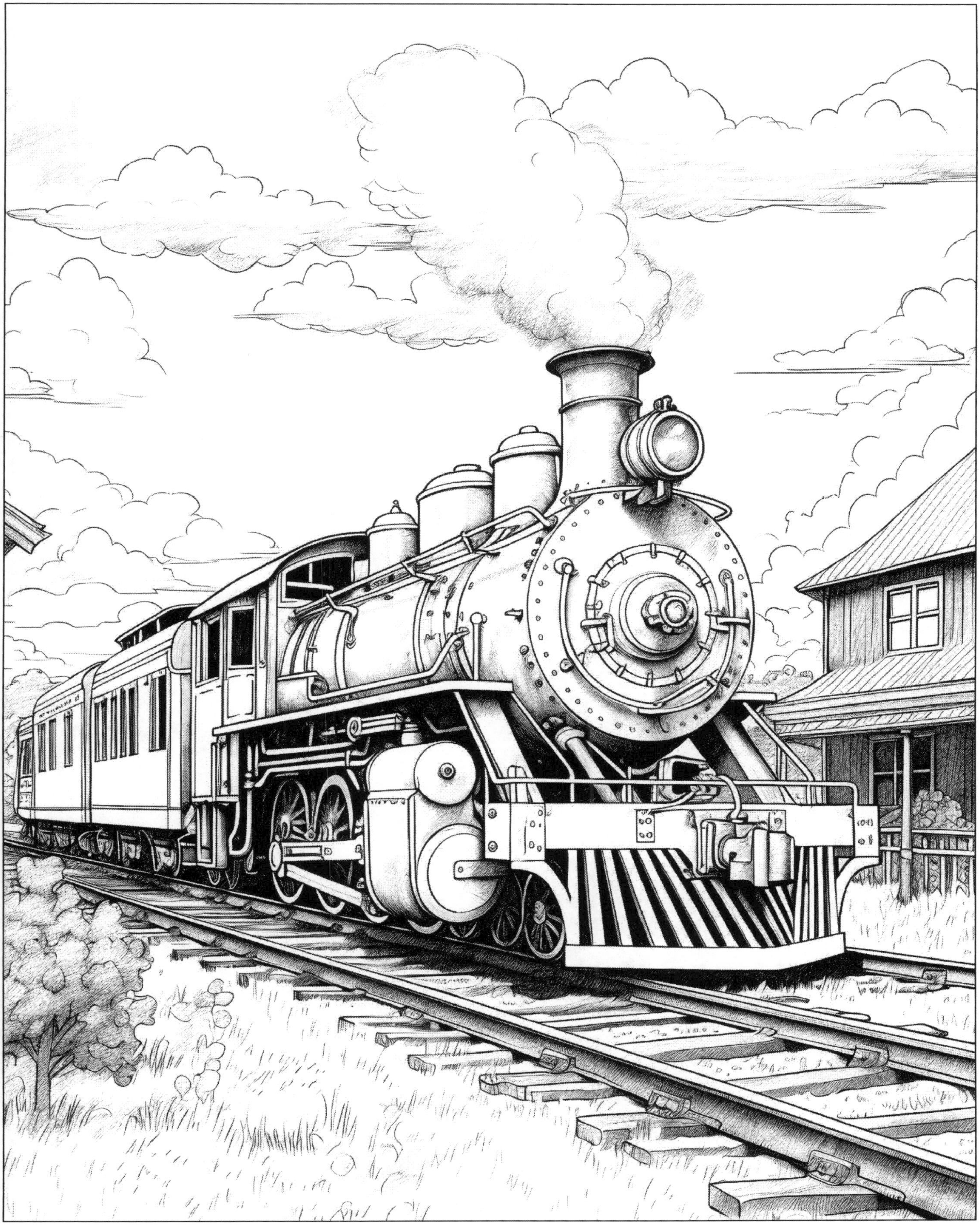

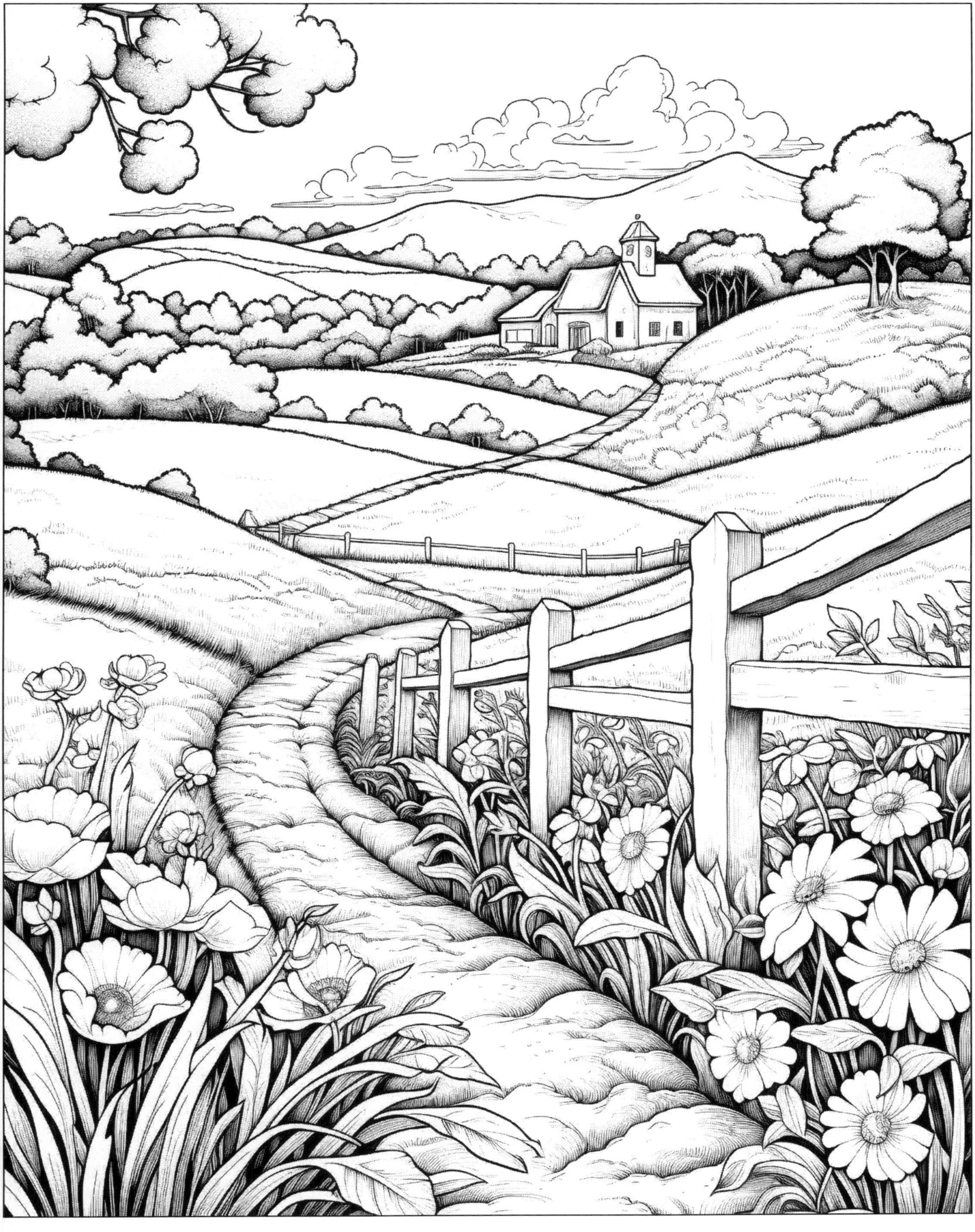

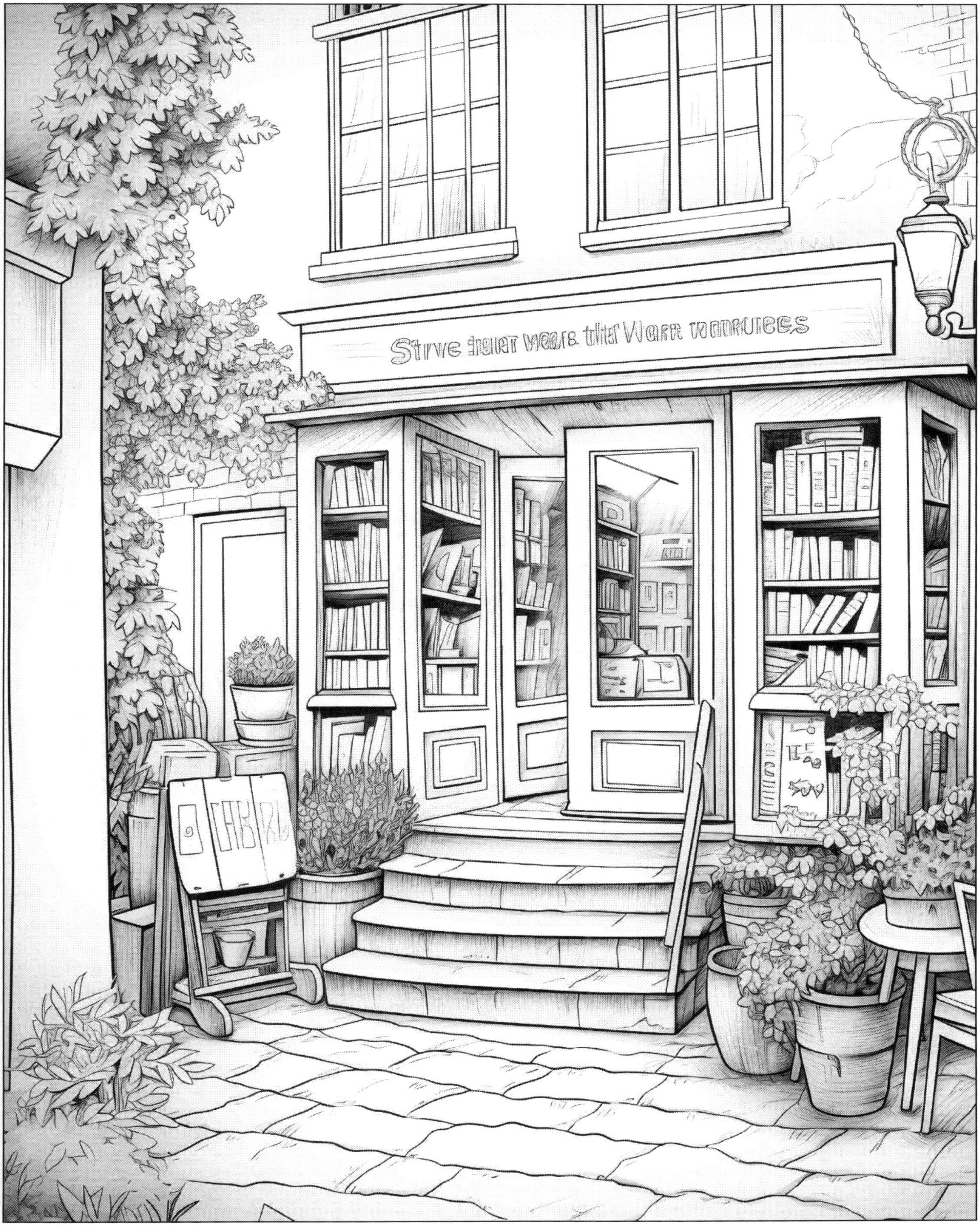

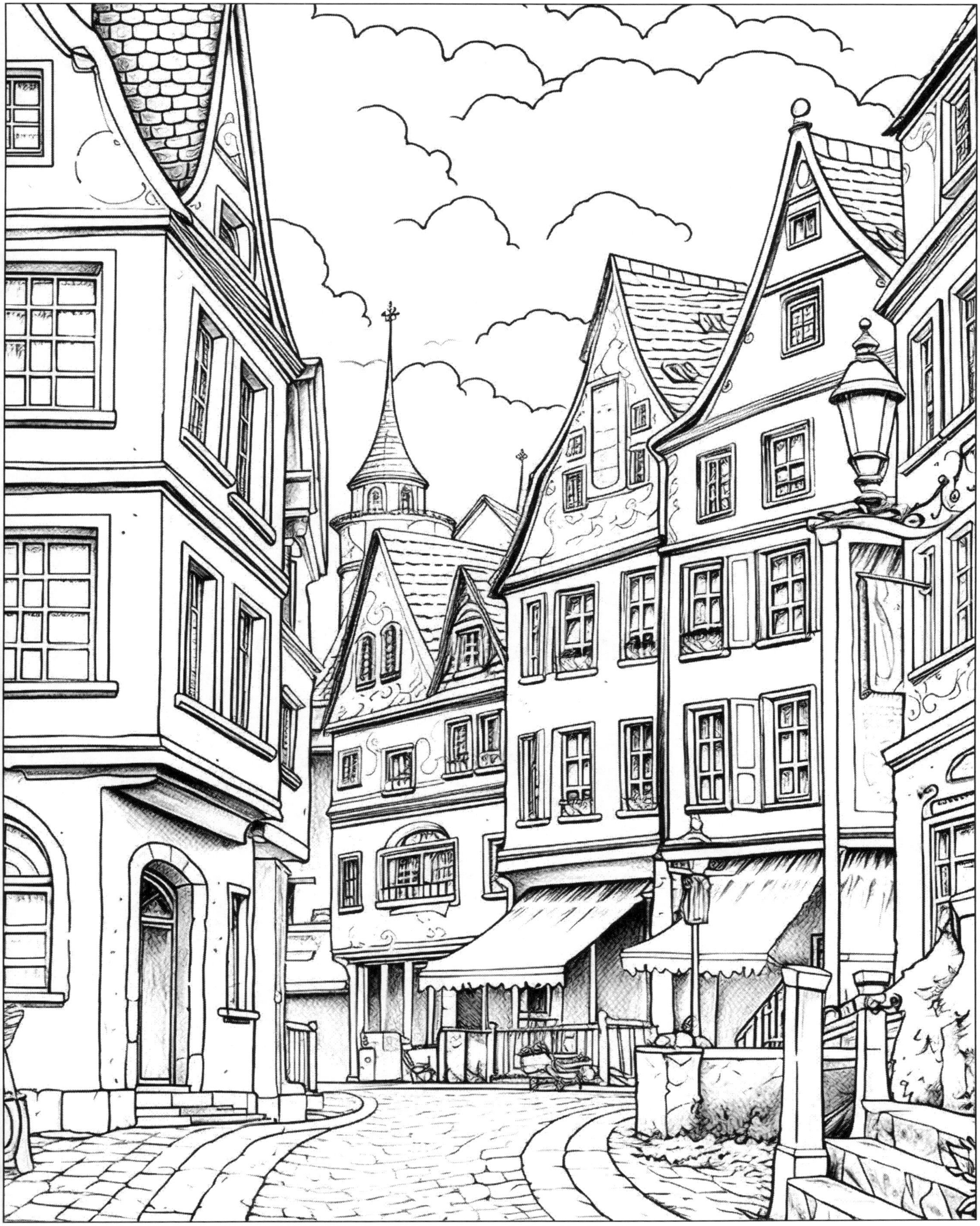

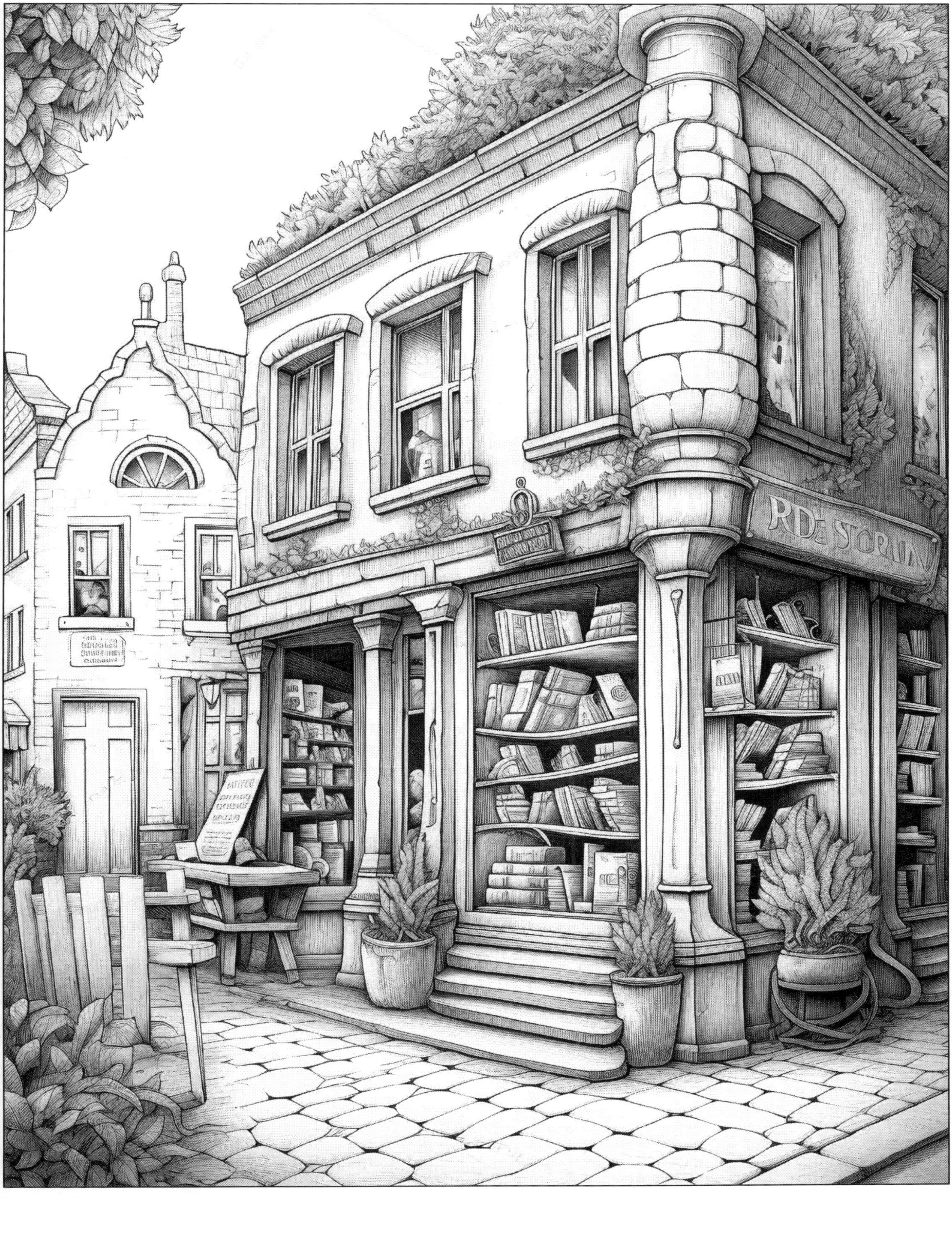

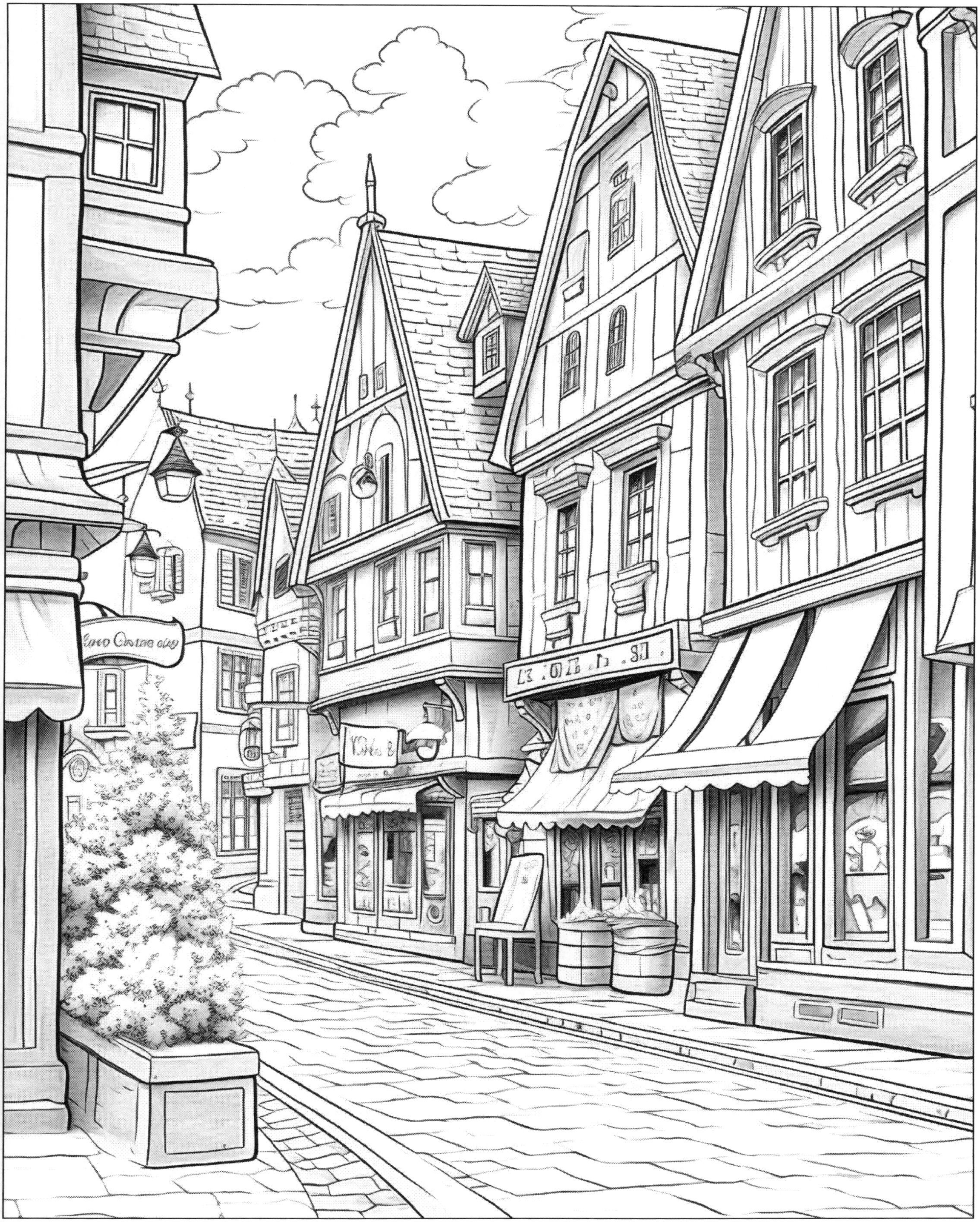

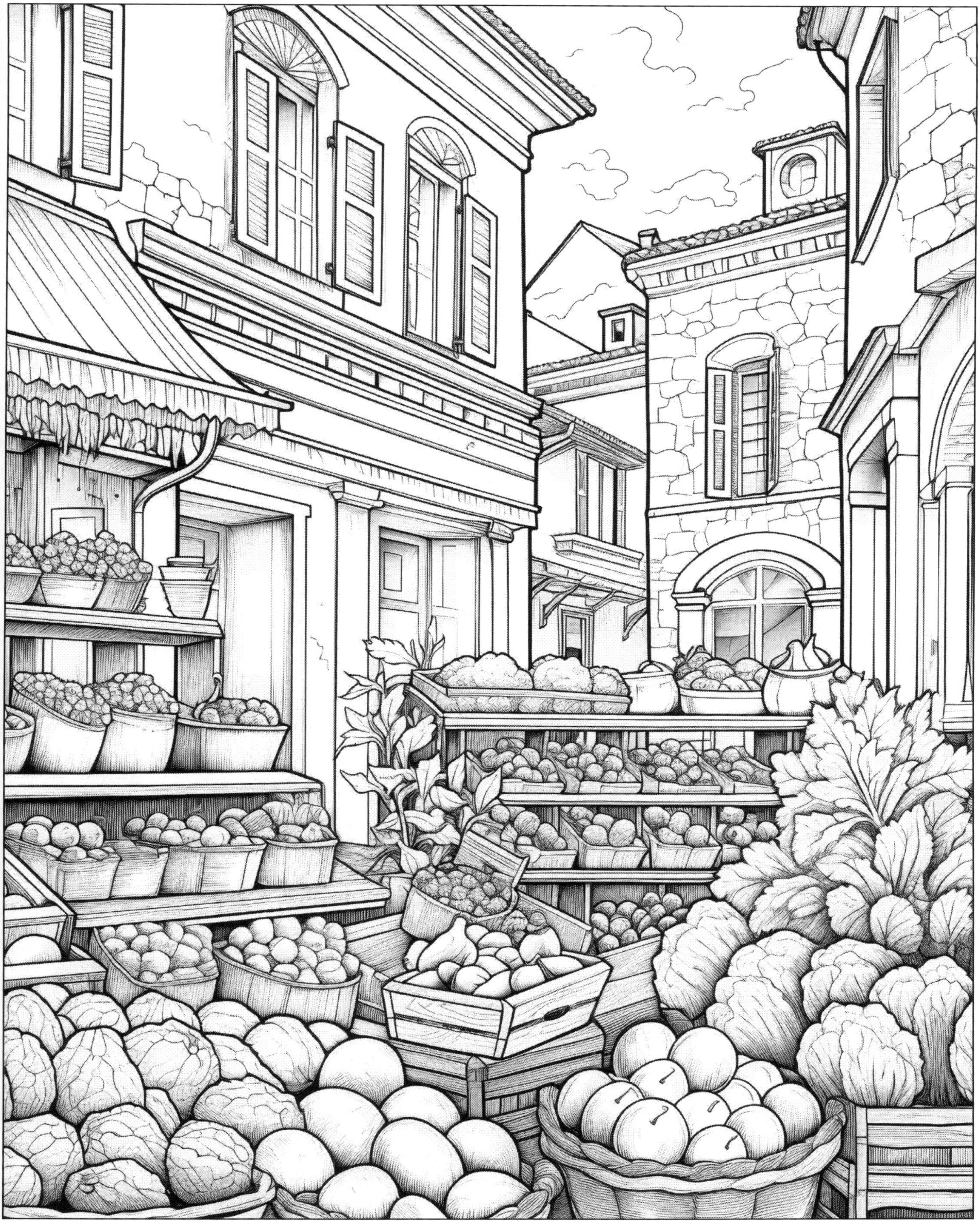

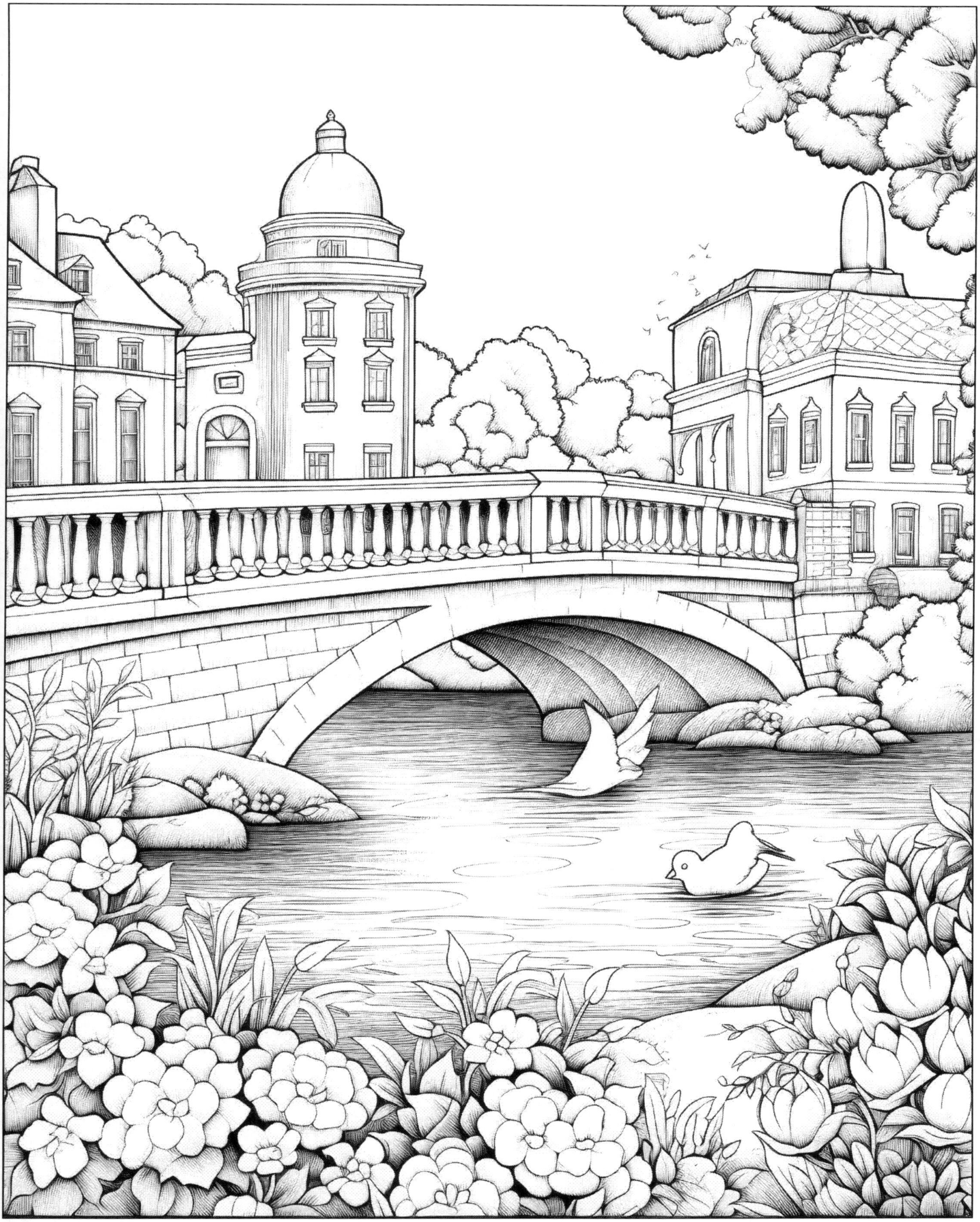

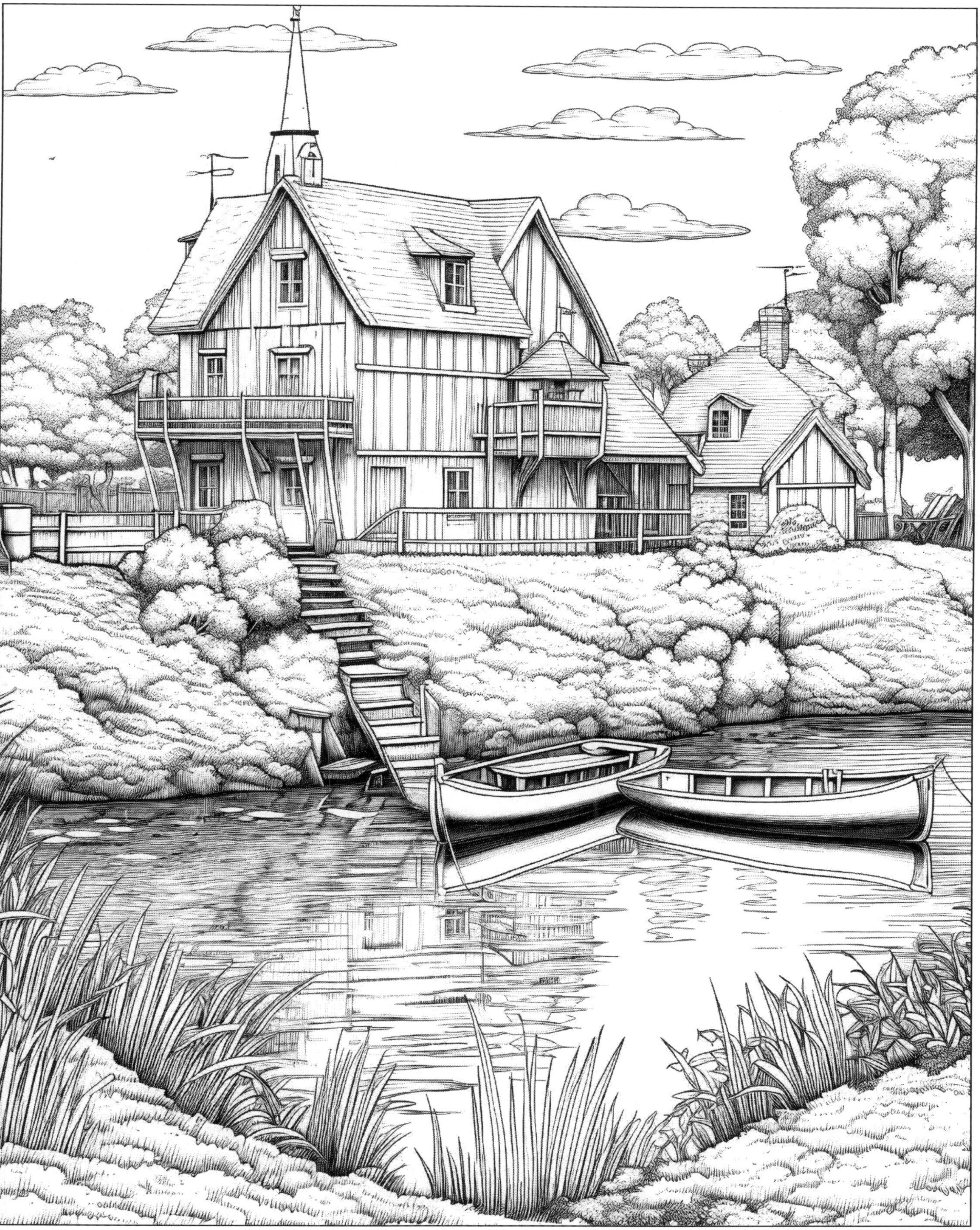

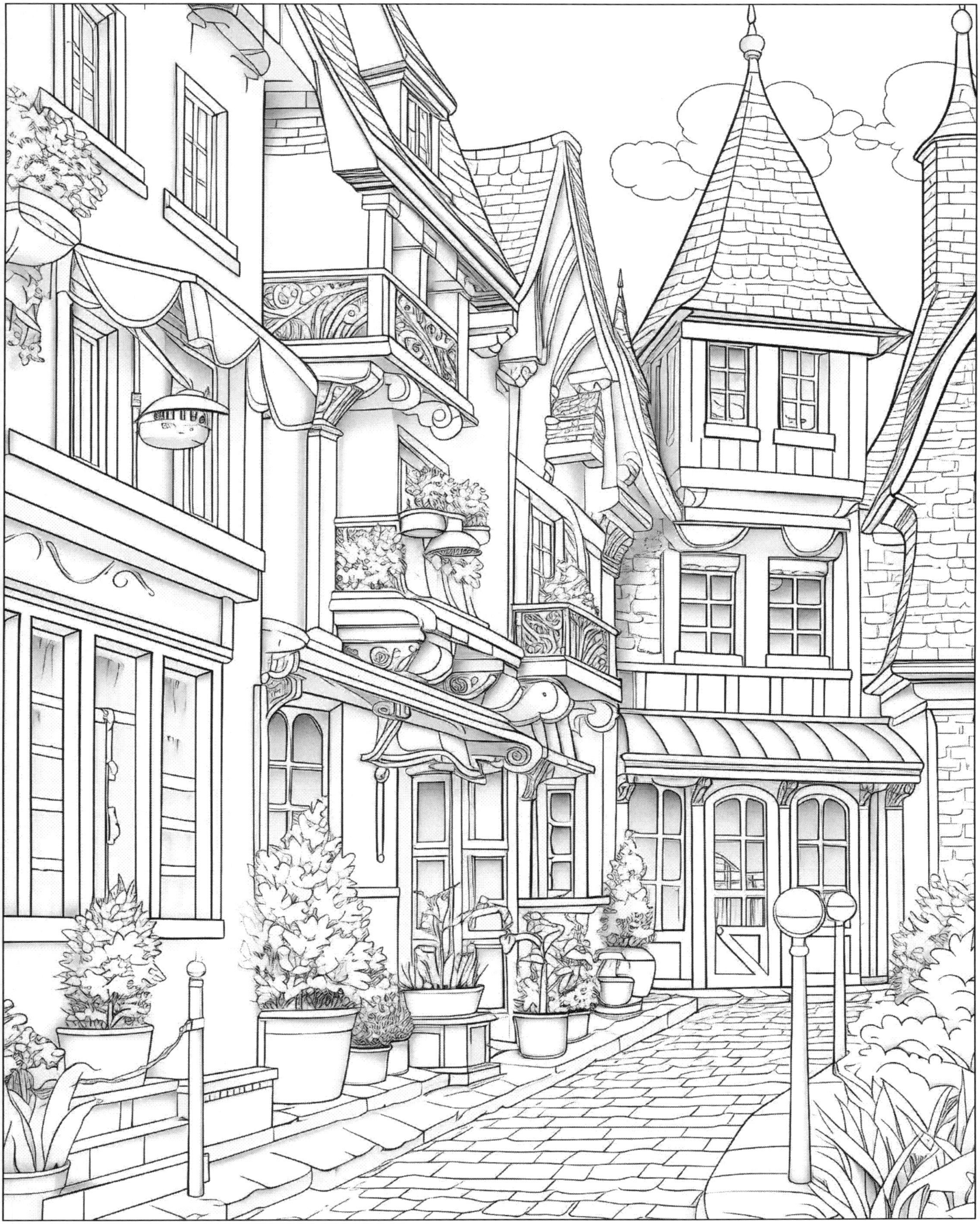

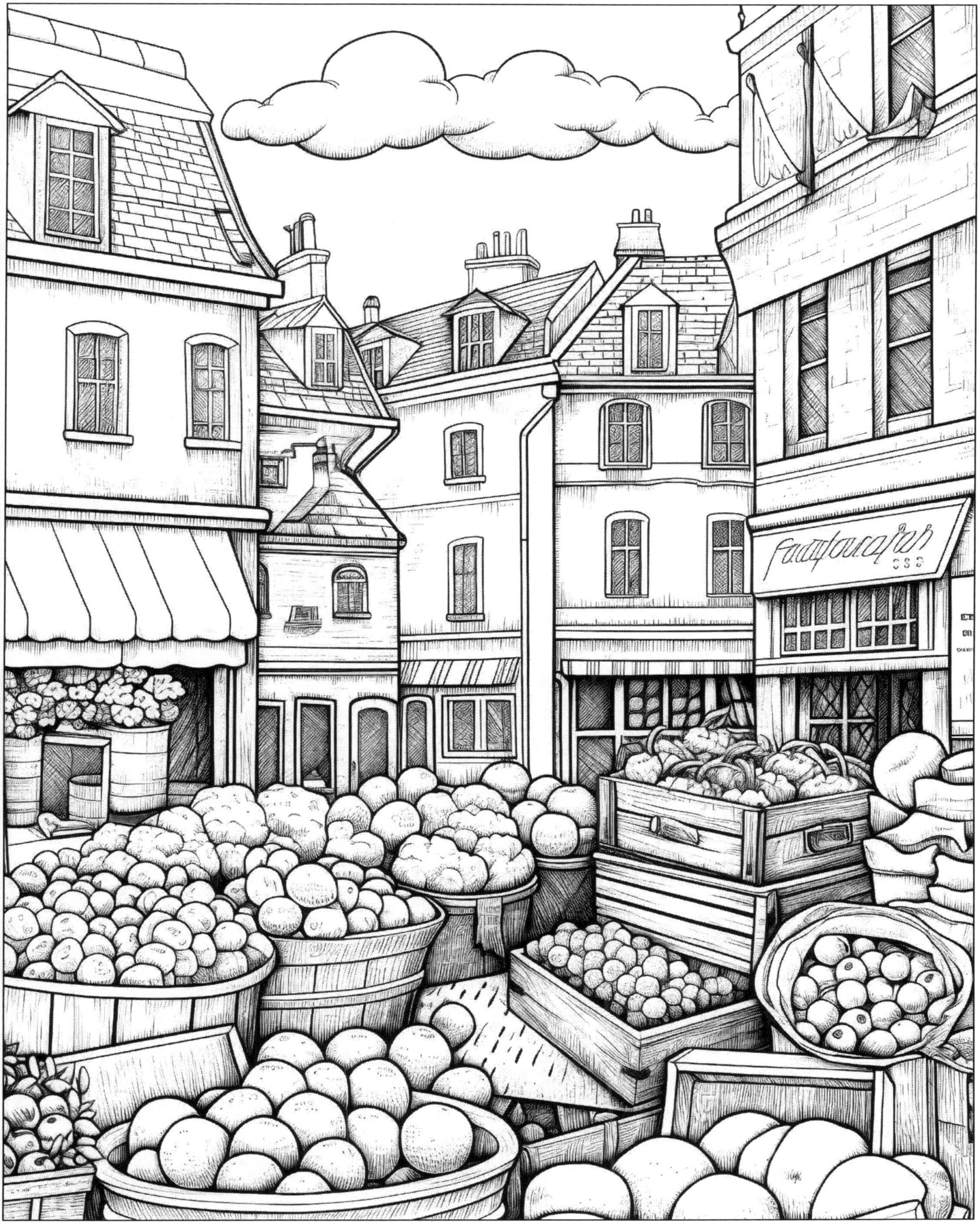

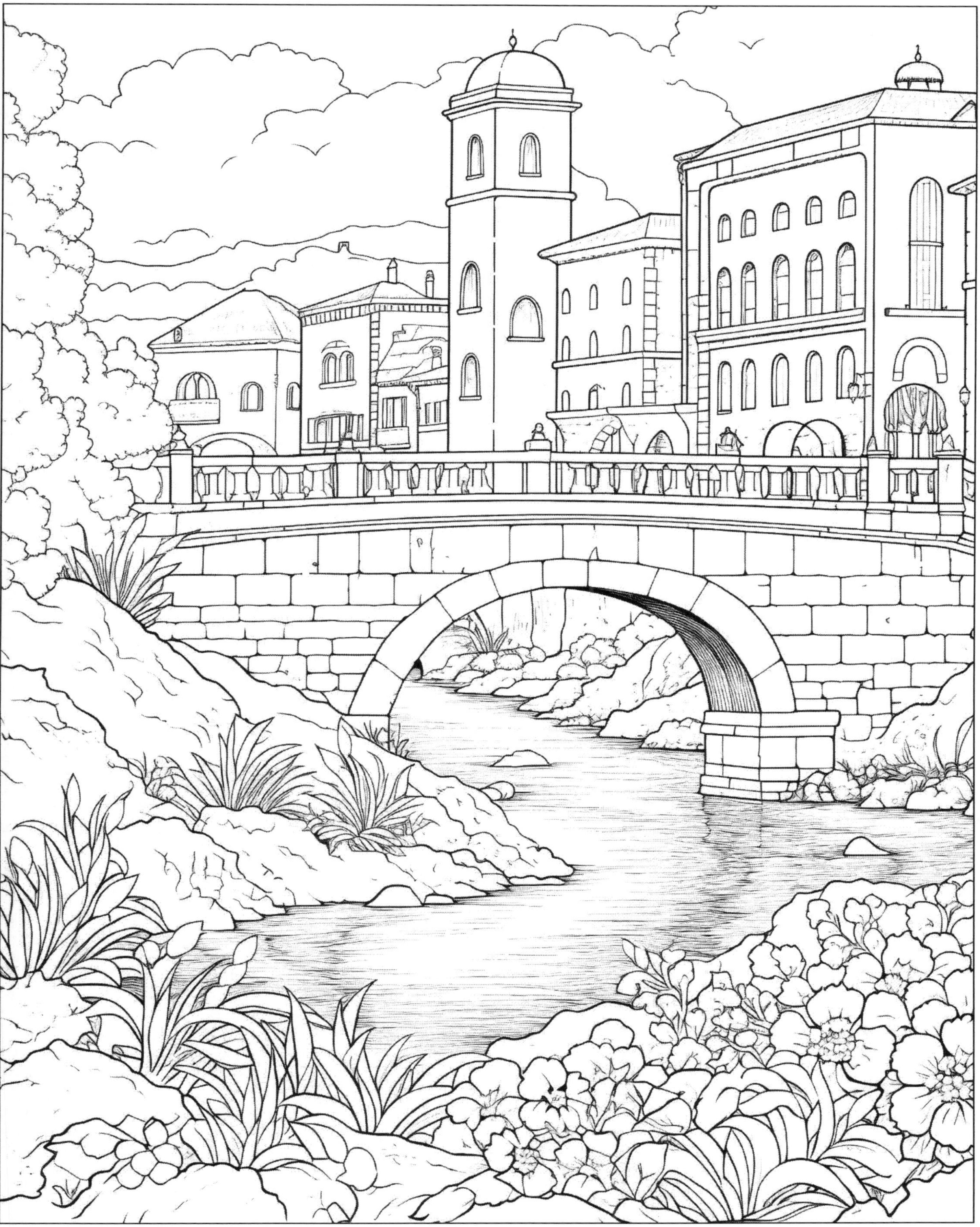

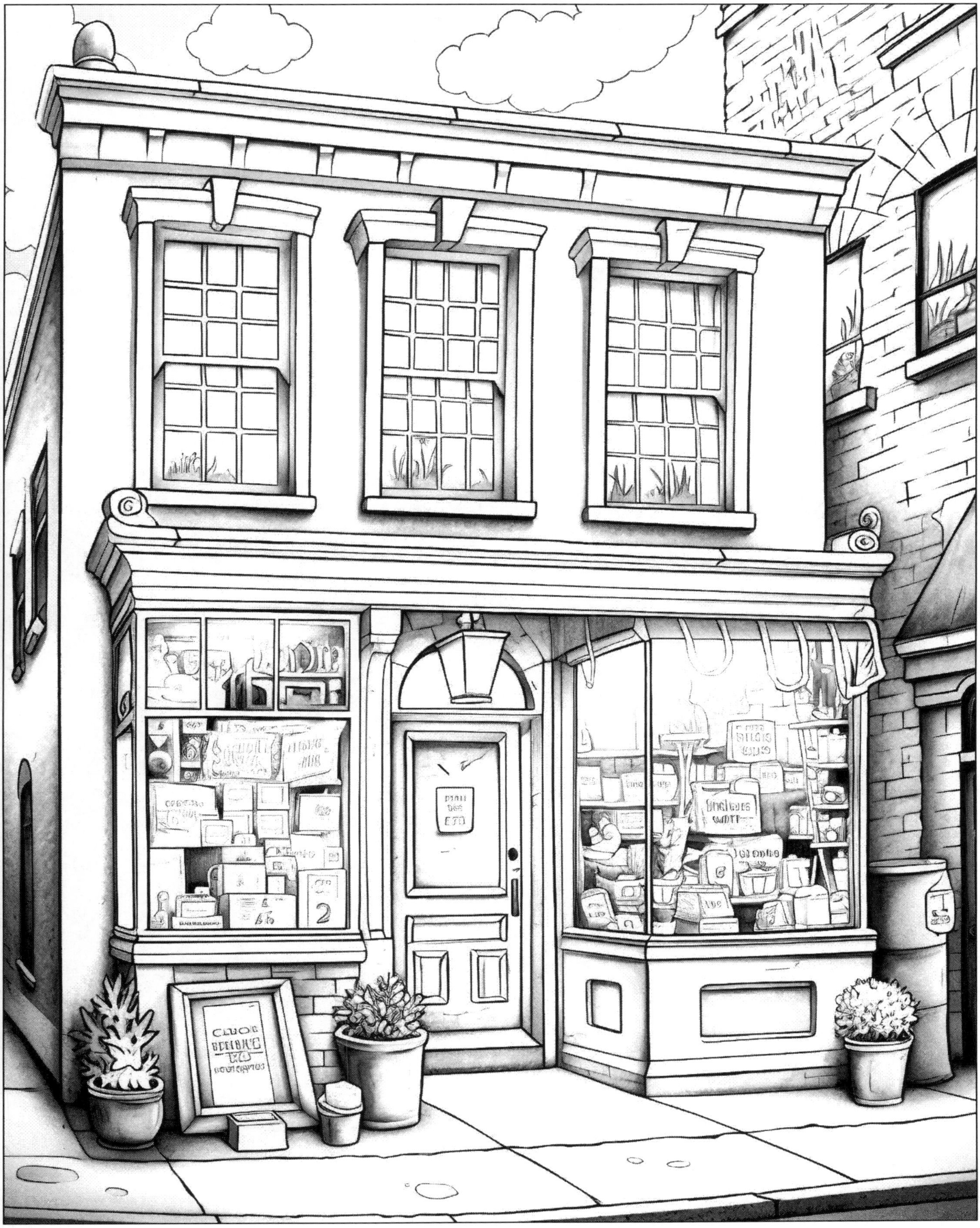

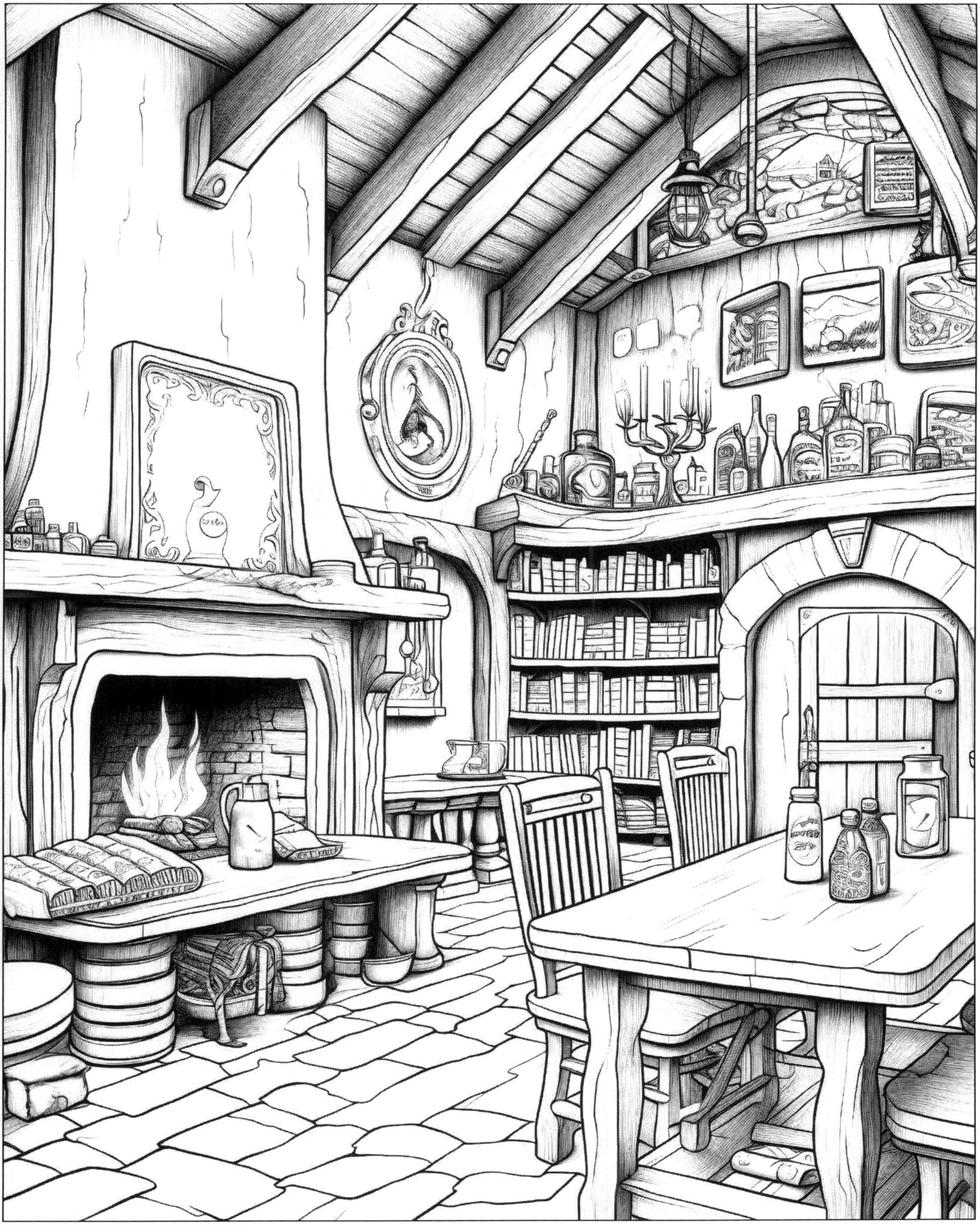

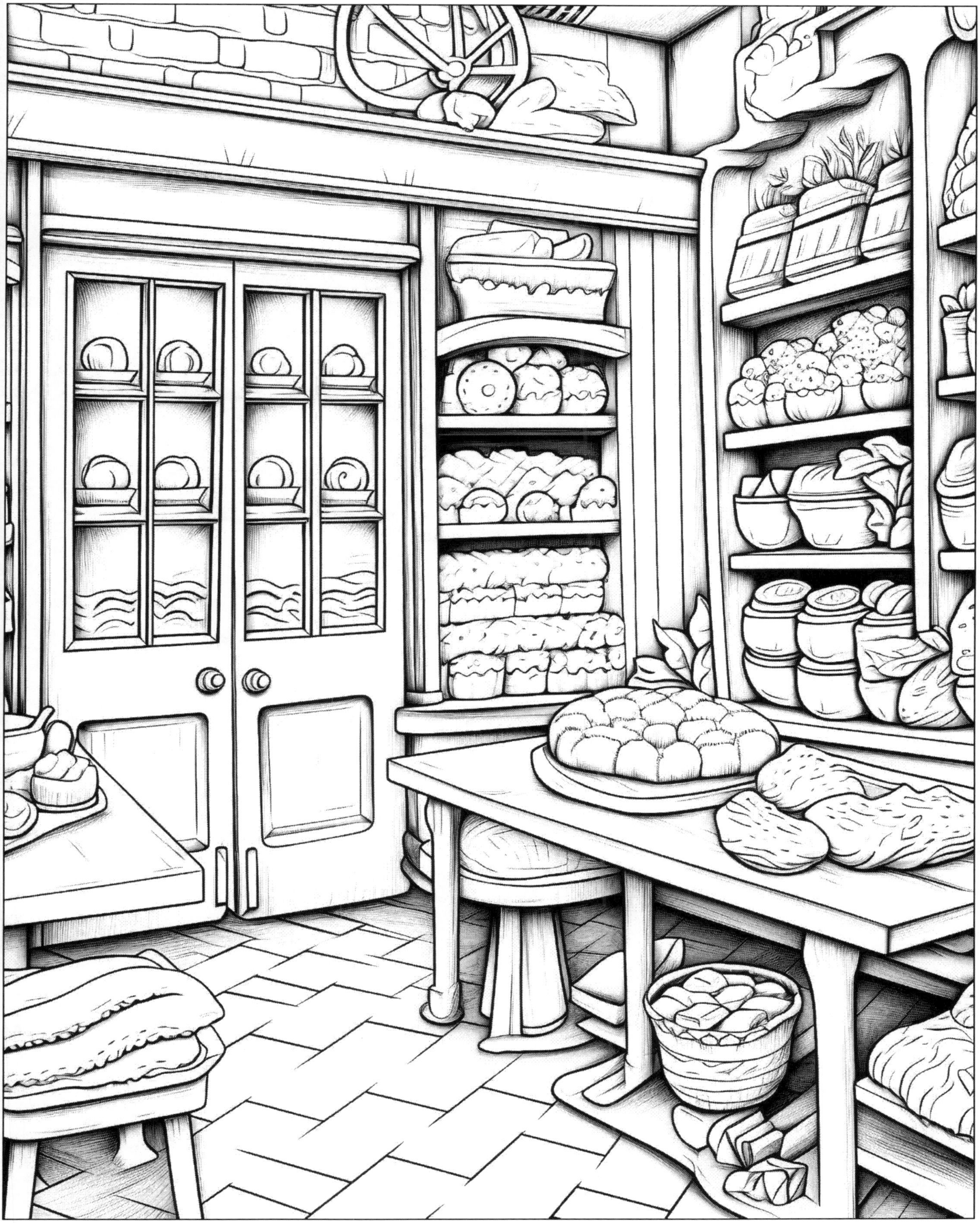

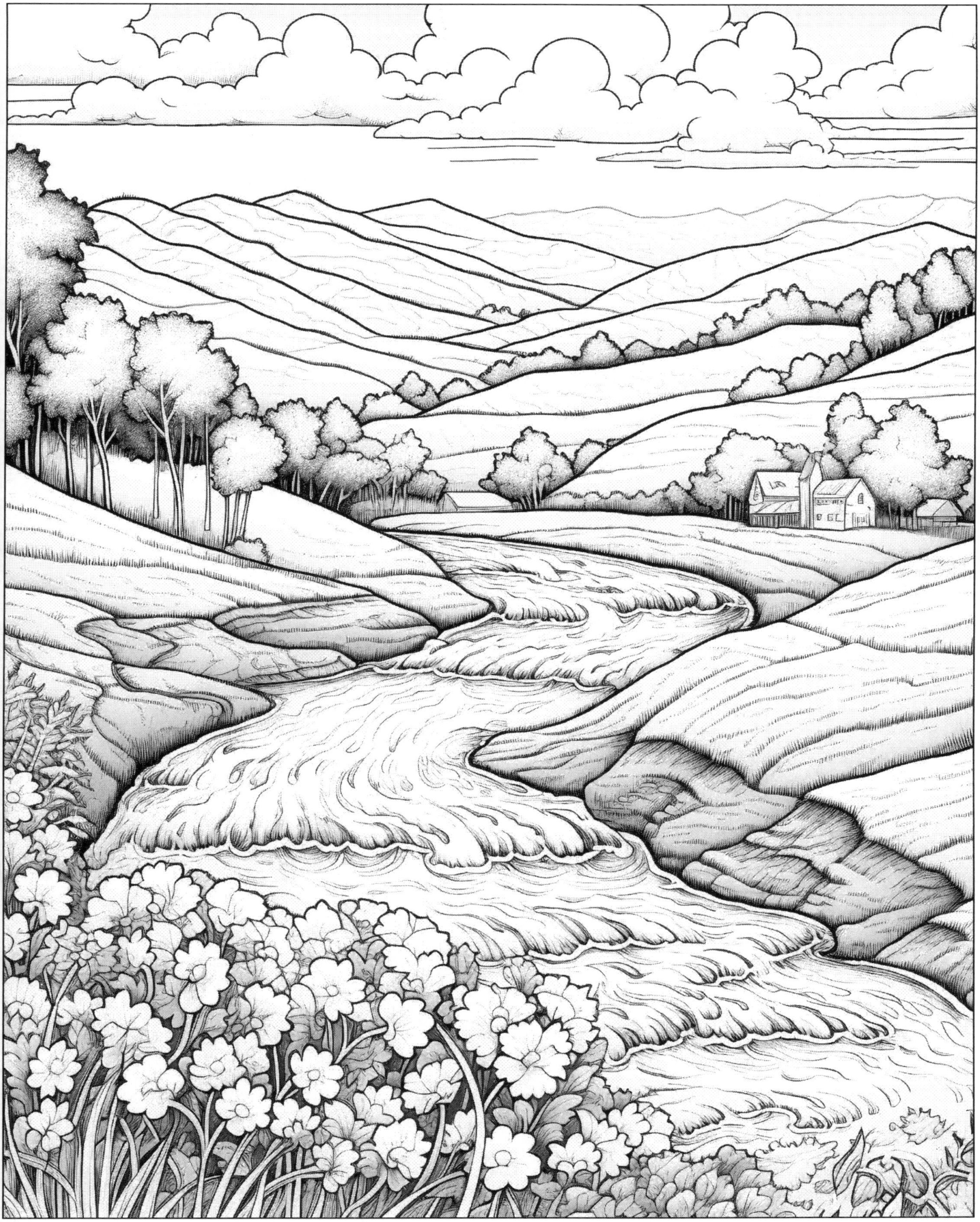

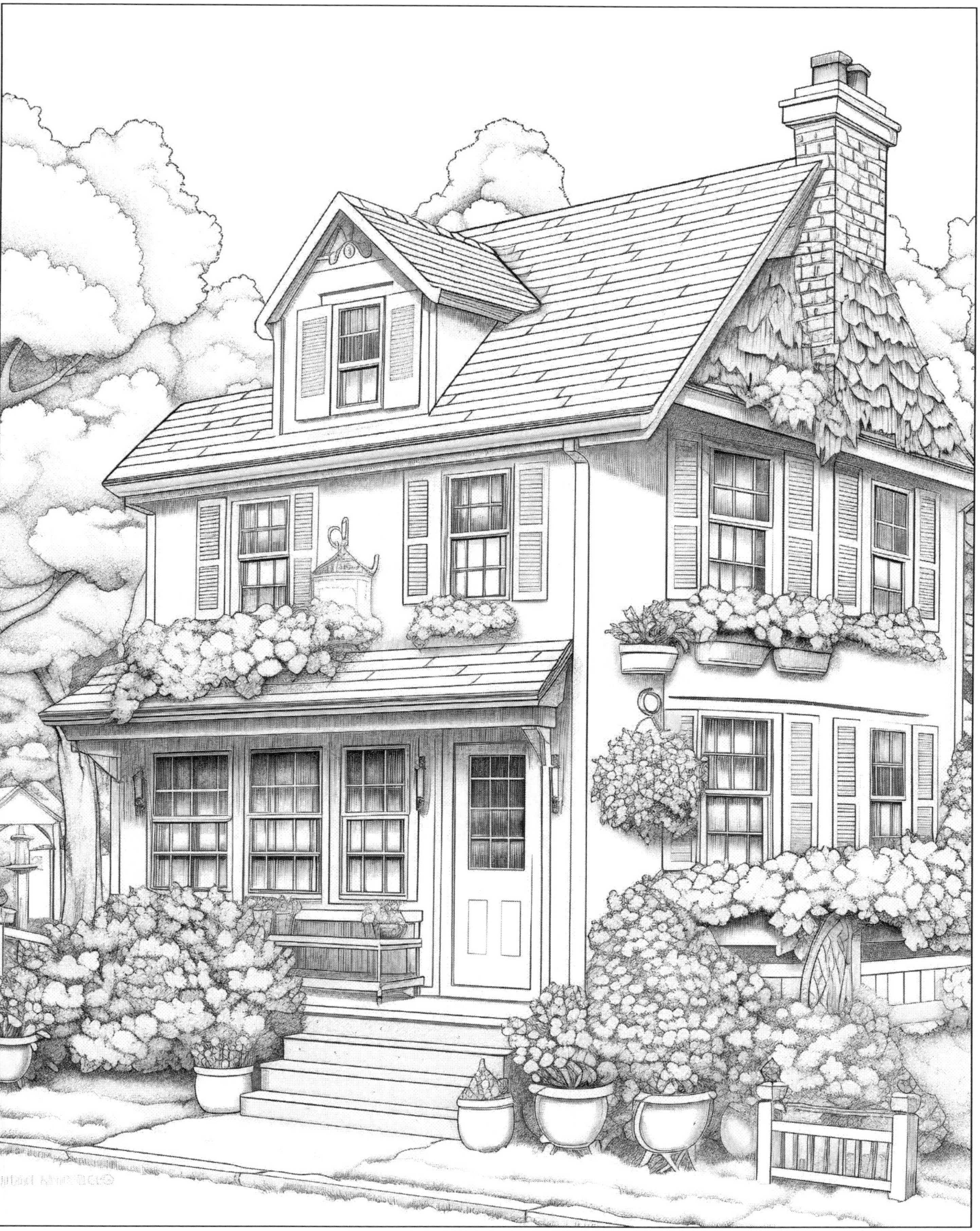

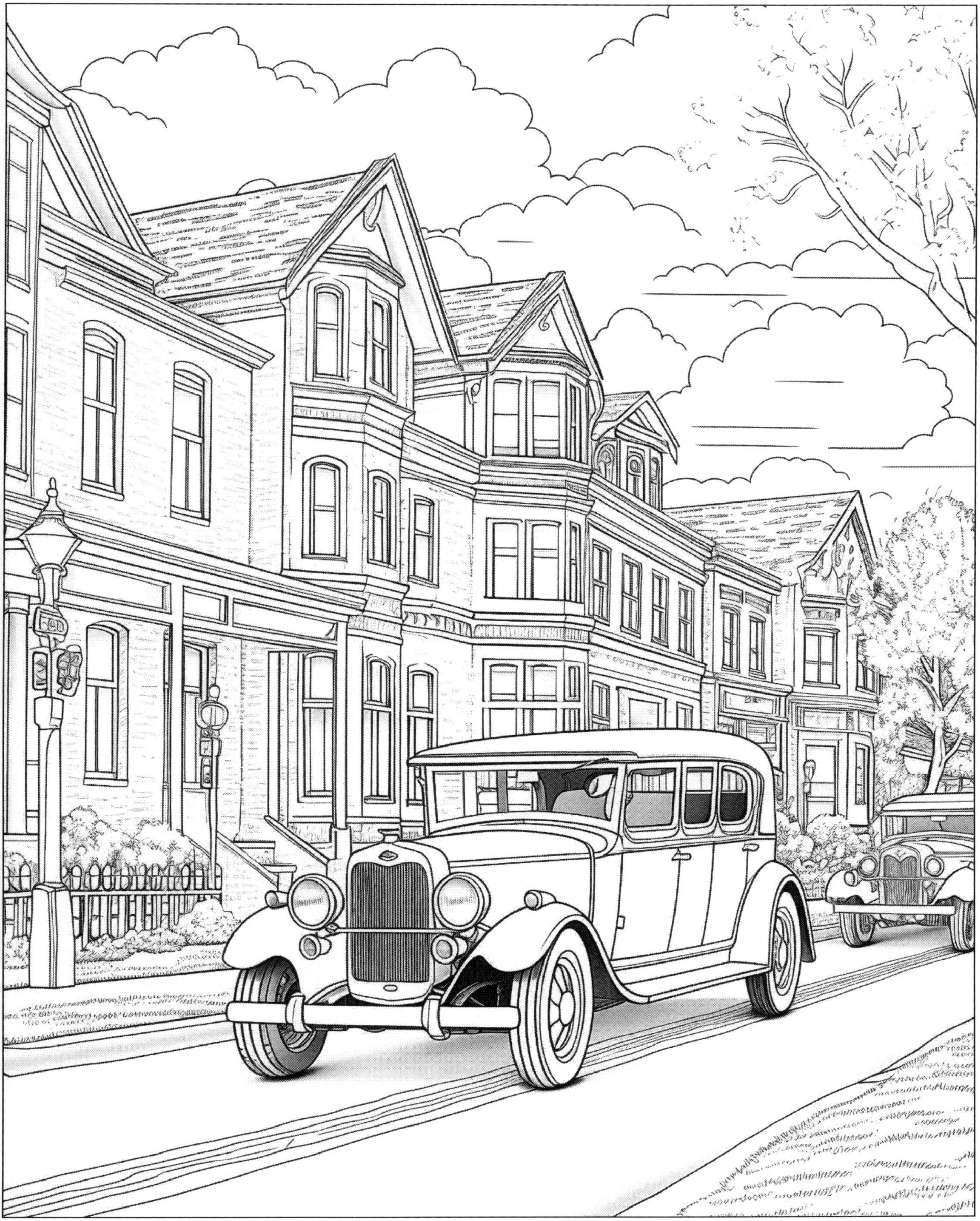

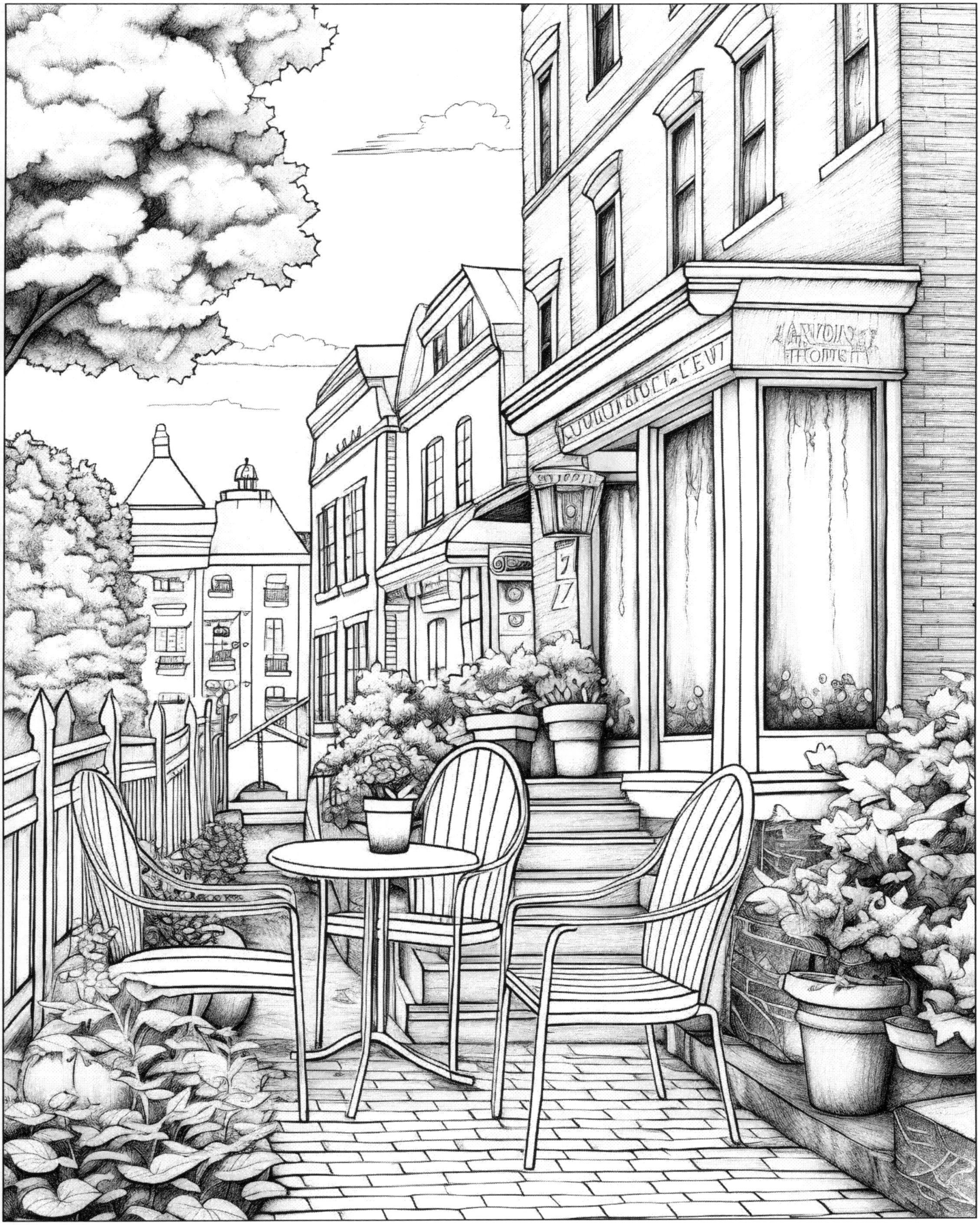

Made in the USA
Las Vegas, NV
28 December 2023

83544118R00059